FACES IN A CLOUD

FACES IN A CLOUD

SUBJECTIVITY IN

PERSONALITY THEORY

Robert D. Stolorow, Ph.D.
and
George E. Atwood, Ph.D.

JASON ARONSON
Northvale, New Jersey
London

Third Printing 1986

ISBN: 0-87668-305-7

Library of Congress Catalog Number: 78-24754

Manufactured in the United States of America

to our parents

CONTENTS

Preface

Chapter 1: **Personality Theory, Metapsychology**   15
            and Subjectivity
  The Observer is the Observed   17
    Subjectivity and Validity • The Psychology and Sociology
    of Knowledge • Decentering in the Genesis of Knowledge
  Attempted Circumventions of Subjectivity   29
    Behaviorism • Methodological Objectivism •
    Phenomenology
  The Case Study Method   39
    The Representational World

Chapter 2: **Sigmund Freud**   47
  Ambivalence in Freud's Life   48
    Earliest Experiences
  Adult Relationships   54
  The Defensive-Restitutive Function of Freud's Theories   63
  Summary and Conclusions   68

Chapter 3: **Carl Jung**   73
  The Representational World in Jung's Theory   73
    The Collective Unconscious and Archetypes •
    Self-Dissolution • The Disunited Man • Individuation
  The Psychological Origins of Jung's Theory   90
    The Genesis of the Secret • Critical Formative
    Experiences • The Subjectivity of Jung's Theories
  Summary and Conclusions   107

Chapter 4: **Wilhelm Reich**   111
  Thematic Structure of Reich's Works   112
    Character Analysis and Orgastic Potency • Political
    Thought • Biological Research and the Treatment of
    Cancer • Unidentified Flying Objects
  A Pivotal Childhood Trauma   119
  Further Aspects of Reich's Life and Thought   122
    Images of History, Civilization, and Nature
  Summary and Conclusions   128

Chapter 5: **Otto Rank**   131
  Rank's Work   132
    The Birth Trauma • The Hero • The Double
    • The Will • Narcissistic Love • Sexual Dread
    and Self-Dissolution • The Artist
  Rank's Life   150
    Evidence of Narcissistic Disturbance • Childhood
    Traumata • Reparative Trends • The Subjectivity of
    Rank's Theories
  Summary and Conclusions   169

Chapter 6: **Psychoanalytic Phenomenology and the
               Psychology of the Representational World**   173
  Critiques of Psychoanalytic Metapsychology   174
  Metapsychology and the Representational World   179
  Toward a Psychoanalytic Phenomenology   182
    Representational Differentiation and Integration •
    Some Common Defenses
  Implications   192
    Psychodiagnosis • Psychoanalytic Therapy • Schools of

Contents

Psychoanalytic Thought • Personality Research • A Procedure for Exploring the Representational World • Metapsychology and Empirical- Phenomenological Personality Research

Index   209

PREFACE

This book is the product of an exceptionally rewarding collaborative endeavor and represents the convergence of several lines of interest. One of us (Atwood) brought to it an interest in the psychology of knowledge, including especially the subjectivity of psychological theorizing. The other (Stolorow) brought a longstanding interest in the possibility of a metapsychology-free framework to guide clinical psychoanalytic conceptualization and treatment. Both of us have shared a feeling of discontent with the current state of personality research and a desire to reintroduce the intensive, in-depth case study as a principal research procedure through which academic personality psychology might rediscover its lost commitment to understanding the experience and conduct of persons. And finally, we are both convinced that an approach which brings to focus and systematically elucidates the nature, significance, and origins of the subjective world of the individual person is the most meaningful one for understanding personality phenomena. These threads of interest are interwoven throughout the book. The contributions which each of us made to the work as a whole were equal in both magnitude and substance. The order of authorship was decided by the toss of a coin.

A number of people have played an important role in the evolution of this book. We wish to express our appreciation first of all to Professor Silvan Tomkins, whose germinal insights into the psychology of knowledge were a continuing source of inspiration for our work. We are also grateful to him for reading the entire manuscript and providing us with incisive criticisms and suggestions.

We are also indebted to Professor Richard Ashmore, Professor Rae Carlson, Dr. James. Fosshage, Dr. Frank Lachmann, Professor Carey McWilliams, Dr. Nancy McWilliams, Professor Daniel Ogilvie, Professor Lawrence Pervin, Professor Seymour Rosenberg, Ms. Mary Lou Tumia, and Dr. Alexander Wolf for reading portions of the work and offering useful and illuminating comments.

We would like to thank Mrs. Virginia Stolorow for performing the tasks of typing, proofreading and editing the manuscript with painstaking devotion, despite being in her ninth month of pregnancy. She was, for her husband, a bountiful source of support, encouragement and tolerance during all phases of this project, and for that he is deeply grateful.

Chapters 2 through 5 of this book are modified and expanded versions of articles which were originally published in psychoanalytic journals: "A Defensive-Restitutive Functions of Freud's Theory of Psychosexual Development," *Psychoanalytic Review* *65(2), 1978;* "Metapsychology, Reification, and the Representational World of C.G. Jung," *International Review of Psycho-Analysis* 4(Part 2), 1977; "The Life and Work of Wilhelm Reich: A Case Study of the Subjectivity of Personality Theory," *Psychoanalytic Review* 64(1), 1977; and "An Ego-Psychological Analysis of the Work and Life of Otto Rank in the Light of Modern Conceptions of Narcissism," *International Review of Psycho-Analysis* 3(Part 4), 1976. We are grateful to the publishers of these journals for granting us permission to reprint substantial portions of the original articles in this work.

Preparation of the manuscript was partially supported by a grant from the Rutgers University Research Council (no. 07—2158).

...man—the object of concern—is like an ever-varying cloud and psychologists are like people seeing faces in it. One psychologist perceives along the upper margin the contours of a nose and lip, and then miraculously other portions of the cloud become so oriented in respect to these that the outline of a forward-looking superman appears. Another psychologist is attracted to a lower segment, sees an ear, a nose, a chin, and simultaneously the cloud takes on the aspect of a backward-looking Epimethean. Thus, for each perceiver every sector of the cloud has a different function, name and value—fixed by his initial bias of perception. To be the founder of a school indeed, it is only necessary to see a face along another margin.

—Henry A. Murray, *Explorations in Personality*

CHAPTER 1

Personality Theory,

Metapsychology and Subjectivity

The modern history of psychology has been marked by the elaboration of divergent theoretical approaches to the understanding of human personality. These include the psychoanalytic and neo-Freudian schools, the humanistic and existential-phenomenological systems, Jungian analytical psychology and Rogerian theory, Reichian and neo-reichian bioenergetics, the numerous behaviorist doctrines deriving from classical conceptions of learning, personal construct theory and factor-analytic frameworks, organismic and field theories, eclectic systems, etc. The relationships among these perspectives are indeterminate and extremely problematic, for each tends to present itself as the foundation for a science of man. This proliferation of theories has not been accompanied by a formulation of principles to guide the assessment of their interrelationships or relative values, and the field as a whole has consequently undergone a process of relentless diversification and fragmentation.

One of the reasons for this diversity and disunity is that these systems for the most part consist not in alternate theoretical models which can be tested against one another in a meaningful way, but rather in competing ideological and conceptual orientations to the problem of what it means to be human. The genuine and in some cases quite profound knowledge established by the different investigators is embedded in irreconcilable, encapsulating structures of metapsychological suppositions. Metapsychology resembles metaphysics in that it preoccupies itself with absolutes and universals. It is a realm of speculative psychological thought far removed from the empirical reality of persons, and aims at knowledge of the ultimate determinants of the human condition. Accordingly, the most divisive controversies within the field of personality theory typically concern not specific empirical phenomena but rather the opposing and hypostatized images of human nature within which those phenomena are interpreted. The concrete knowledge of persons at the heart of the different theories is thus obscured by their more visible conceptualizations of man in universal terms.

Personality theorists are traditionally not satisfied with conducting empirical studies of the vicissitudes of sexual life, for example, but instead feel impelled to conceptualize objective drives or bioenergies from which sexual experiences are presumed to derive (Freud, Reich); the discovery of intriguing correspondences between the spontaneous symbolic imagery of individuals and the imagery of collective myths gives way to the postulation of the existence of inherited, transpersonal regions of the psyche (Jung); and the elucidation of defensive and reparative techniques used by certain individuals to master the dread of death and self-dissolution becomes transformed into a reified, universalized conception of human motivation (Rank). In our view, metapsychological thought is symptomatic of the difficulties psychology has had in defining itself as an independent discipline. On the one hand, its speculative absolutes of human nature are reminiscent of metaphysics and reflect the continuing lack of differentiation between psychology and philosophy. Its preoccupation with universal laws and quasi-objective energies and its inclination to treat immaterial subjective experiences as thinglike entities, on the other hand, import imagery from the physical and biological sciences and reflect the failure of personality theory to define concepts and units of analysis in its own psychological and phenomenological terms.

While the existence of metapsychology is associated with the struggles of psychology to establish itself as an independent field, the specific configurations of its various conflicting doctrines derive from other sources. We believe that their most powerful source can be found in the subjective experiential worlds of the personality theorists themselves. It is our contention that the subjective world of the theorist is inevitably translated into his metapsychological conceptions and hypotheses regarding human nature, limiting the generality of his theoretical constructions and lending them a coloration expressive of his personal existence as an individual. This book is concerned with the subjectivity of psychological knowledge and especially with the subjective origins of universalized metapsychological doctrines. We shall present analyses of four major personality theorists from a psychobiographical perspective. By systematically interpreting the theories as psychological products embedded in the context of life history and personal phenomenology, we hope to deepen our understanding of the limiting role of these subjective factors. We further intend to use the psychobiographical analyses as points of departure for a discussion of the possibility of a more general and inclusive framework for understanding human personality.

THE OBSERVER IS THE OBSERVED

Every theory of personality constitutes a system of statements regarding the meaning of being human in the world. Each theory is founded upon distinctive images of the human condition and the essential relationships between man and the world. These images are, at least in part, subjective and pretheoretical in origin; rather than being results of impartial reflection upon empirical facts accessible to everyone, they are bound up with the theorist's personal reality and precede his intellectual engagement with the problem of human nature. The personality theorist is a person and therefore views the world from the limited perspective of his own subjectivity. His understanding of the phenomena of human behavior develops within certain limiting dimensions of experience which are themselves the products of his particular life history. This is true of anyone's view of man and the world, but it leads to a profound dilemma in the psychology of personality. Jung has observed of this situation that "in psychology the means by which you study the psyche is the psyche itself.... The observer is the observed. The psyche is not only the object, but also the subject of our science" (1968, pp. 41–42). If psychologists were transcendent beings capable of viewing the world from a standpoint of unconditioned objectivity, they could approach the study of the human condition unaffected by factors that are a part of the very phenomena they are seeking to understand. Since this is not the case, however, all theories of personality will remain colored by subjective and personal influences.

Personality theorists tend to rely on their own lives as a primary source of empirical material. Obviously true of Freud and Jung, both of whom conducted intensive self-analyses, it holds also for the creators of other systems, even those of a nonanalytic nature. No theorist offers definitive statements on the meaning of being human unless he feels those statements constitute a framework within which he can comprehend his own experience. One might imagine that self-analysis and self-study would diminish the influence of subjective factors on theory-building, by alerting the theorist to the particularity of his own perspective. Actually, this is true only to a very limited extent. The explorations and reconstructions of self-analysis filter one's life history through an interpretive nexus which is partially that life history's own product, and the results of self-analysis are inevitably affected by the experiential world in which it is embedded.

The present-day lack of consensus in psychology as to basic conceptual frameworks is partially the product of these subjective and personal influences. It is not simply that each theory is the expression of the limits and biases of the theorist, but also that other persons, in their reactions to theoretical ideas, are similarly subject to these influences. The act of familiarizing oneself with an intellectual system dealing with the nature of man and the essential problems of human existence is a complex cognitive and emotional experience. A person's commitment to a particular personality theory is therefore a process rather different from what the popular canons of scientific method would lead one to believe. These canons conceive of the acceptance of a theory, or the rejection of it, in exclusively rational terms; they emphasize that acceptance or rejection is governed by a dispassionate evaluation of the system's logical coherence and consistency with empirical reality. In actuality, the process is considerably more involved. A serious confrontation with a theory of personality awakens a whole pattern of positive and negative subjective resonance in the individual, and his eventual attitudes toward the material will be profoundly affected by its degree of compatibility with his own personal reality. One might even say that the evaluation of a personality theory approximates the prevailing ideology of science only to the extent that, for reasons again rooted in subjectivity, the individual seeks to identify himself with the image of disinterested objectivity and rationality.

Consider, for example, the probable impact of a deterministic standpoint such as that of behaviorism on a person for whom the preservation of a sense of autonomy is felt to be necessary. Clearly, his negative reaction will powerfully influence his attitude toward the behaviorist school of thought, matters of logic and evidence aside. Or conversely, suppose that a theory such as Sartrean ontology, which postulates the radical freedom of the subject, confronts an individual for whom the systematic denial of agency and freedom is necessary to master an otherwise unbearable sense of responsibility and guilt. Consider the sudden, conversionlike enchantments with various systems which can often be observed, whereby a group of theoretical ideas seemingly becomes incorporated as a whole new mode of representing existence. Consider also the equally sudden disenchantments which may occur. Envision the intriguing problem of the subjective determinants underlying the tendency of certain students and scholars to resonate simultaneously to opposed, irreconcilable theoretical standpoints, or in the course of their careers to swing dramatically from one ideological and theoretical extreme to another. Herein lies a field rich in research problems, and one which has hardly even begun to be explored (see Tomkins 1965, Coan 1973, Atwood and Tomkins 1976).

The modern field of personality psychology comprises a variety of schools of thought, each of which carries on research within its own limited domain, more or less oblivious to the contributions and discoveries made from other theoretical positions. As a result, psychological research on human personality is largely a noncumulative affair. This is in contrast to the natural sciences, where knowledge develops in a progressively accumulating and deepening way. Investigations in physics, chemistry and biology proceed by building on the concepts and findings of previous theory and research. The psychology of personality tends, by contrast, to ignore its own history, constantly making fresh starts with the introduction of new paradigms and viewpoints. One of the reasons for this unfortunate state of affairs is that there is no theory of personality sufficiently general to include and unify the various schools of thought.

A truly unifying theory of personality ought to be able to account not only for the phenomena that all other theories address, but also for these theories themselves. This is so because each of these constructions is a psychological product which embodies a pretheoretical subjective vision rooted in the theorist's own development as a person. In this respect, the psychology of personality differs radically from other sciences. In the disciplines of natural science there is a sharp boundary between explanatory systems on the one hand and empirical phenomena on the other. A physical theory, for example, need only account for physical phenomena; there is no obligation to also account for competing theories. In the field of personality psychology the explanatory systems are a part of the empirical domain.

If the science of human personality is ever to achieve a greater degree of consensus and generality, it must turn back on itself and question its own psychological foundations. There must be sustained study not only of the phenomena which have always been its province, but also of the biasing subjective factors which contribute to its continuing diversity and fragmentation. Progress toward clarifying these predisposing influences can be achieved by a psychobiographical method which systematically interprets the metapsychological ideas of personality theories in light of the critical formative experiences in the respective theorists' lives. By elucidating the ways in which theoretical ideas are conditioned by the personality of the theorist, this interpretive process transforms the subjectivity inherent in present systems into an explicit object of investigation. Psychobiography cannot, of course, lead directly to a reconciliation of the different theories, nor to the creation of a more general framework. Its value lies rather in explicating a group of factors which limit the generality of existing concepts and contribute to a continuing proliferation of divergent viewpoints.

It might appear that this kind of work creates a paradox, in that the proposed interpretations might depend, like the mythical snake that devours itself by swallowing its own tail, on concepts from the very theories being analyzed. We believe this paradox is more apparent than real. The psychological analysis of a personality theory is not an attempt to explain away its concepts but rather to assess and understand the theorist's underlying vision. Moreover, the psychobiographical method need not restrict itself to the use of only those concepts which are at the same time being analyzed. On the contrary, it should be capable of flexibly drawing upon the knowledge of all the different schools of thought, and also of devising new concepts as it goes along.

Subjectivity and Validity

There are two problems associated with the study and clarification of the subjective origins of personality theory. The first of these is entirely empirical in character, i.e., the problem of identifying the personal influences which can actually be shown to color a theorist's thought. This empirical task may pass over into the second problem, which concerns the import of the subjective dimension for assessing the validity of the theory. One position which may be taken regarding this relationship would be to consider the explication of psychological origins as a means of invalidating the theory. For anyone who has familiarized himself with the power of psychobiographical analysis and knows of the extensive, intricately structured ways in which a theorist's work is infiltrated by his personal reality, this position can seem persuasive. We nevertheless consider it untenable, for to construe such an analysis as an invalidation would be to subvert the logic of the entire enterprise of personality theory. Investigations of the subjective origins of knowledge are themselves associated with a background of subjectivity and can in principle be analyzed and "invalidated" in the same manner.

In opposition to the reductionism of this first position is the far more prevalent notion that the issue of origins and the issue of validity are entirely separate problems which have no bearing on each other. The validity of a theory must be determined in ways sharply dissociated from considerations of genesis. In the context of our present studies, according to this line of argument, the illumination of personal worlds underlying the different theories, although perhaps interesting as particular case studies, contributes precisely nothing to the assessment of their value as explanatory systems. Although this position avoids the logical fallacy of a thoroughgoing reductionism, it creates what we believe is an unnecessary and intellectually deadening conceptual barrier between the theorist as a person and the products of his work. Indeed, the isolation of considerations of origin from problems of validity reinforces the continuing blindness of professional psychologists to the profound and multifaceted ways in which they are implicated in their own research.

The ultimate aim of personality theory is to arrive at comprehensive principles to account for human experience and human conduct. But the empirical phenomena of the human world present themselves differently according to the perspective of the observer. The particularity of the psychological context from which the personality theorist views reality guarantees that his interpretations will be focused on selected features of the empirical field, and that the specific dimensions of human conduct bearing a correspondence to his own pretheoretical vision of man will be magnified in his eventual theoretical constructions. The potential for achieving for our knowledge a truly general validity is therefore rather sharply circumscribed by the subjective factors we have been discussing. It would be incorrect to view an explication of the personal realities embedded in psychological theories as giving no more than an account of the conditions of their genesis. Every thorough psychobiographical analysis delimits, in content as well as origin, the view being studied. It seeks not only to establish a relationship between the theorist and his works, but also to determine the particularization of scope of the theory, and hence to delimit its generality and validity (see Mannheim 1936, for a parallel discussion of validity and the *social* determinants of knowledge).

Our position on the relationship between subjectivity and validity is thus different from the two views discussed above. The analysis of origins, while not constituting an invalidation, assists in the demarcation of generality and also in the mapping of the field to be accounted for by more embracing theories (see Mannheim 1936). We envision a hierarchical progression of recursive analyses, in which the theoretical systems at each level of the hierarchy are shown to be limited and particularized by reference to the more inclusive systems at succeeding levels.

There is yet another respect in which studies of subjective origins bear on the problem of validity. As will be discussed more fully in later chapters, personality theories contain many concepts which cannot under any circumstances be validated (or invalidated); these are the reified metapsychological superstructures presumed to encompass and ultimately to determine the human condition. Among such concepts are Freud's drive theory, Jung's notion of the collective or transpersonal unconscious, Reich's theory of the orgone bioenergy, and Rank's conception of the Will. Careful study of ways in which these and certain other metapsychological constructs were used by the personality theorists shows that they are such highly speculative, experience-distant conceptualizations that no decisive check of their empirical validity is possible. It is precisely at the level of these reified images that the subjectivity of the theorist becomes most apparent, for they can be shown to vividly reflect his personal solutions to the nuclear crises of his own life history.

The Psychology and Sociology of Knowledge

The psychobiographical investigation of personality theory actually represents only one branch of a broader discipline which would study the role of subjective factors in the structure of man's knowledge in general. Following Tomkins (1965), we can call this broader discipline "the psychology of knowledge." This would concern itself with knowledge which is demonstrably valid, knowledge which is demonstrably invalid, and knowledge which is based on faith. It would also concern itself with the ebb and flow of emotional investments in ideas and ideology, in methods and styles of investigation, and in what are considered acceptable criteria of evidence. It would study subjective and personal influences on artistic and literary creations, philosophical systems and political theories, and on works in the sciences and mathematics as well. This discipline would be reflexive in structure, i.e., one of its branches would be devoted to understanding the subjective origins of studies and interests in the psychology of knowledge itself.

A strong analogy exists between the issues studied in the "psychology of knowledge" and those studied in the "sociology of knowledge." The dependence of intellectual activity upon its social and historical environment was recognized by Marx and Weber, but it was first explicitly studied by Karl Mannheim (1936, 1952). Mannheim distinguished between *immanent* and *extrinsic* perspectives on intellectual systems and ideologies. From the immanent perspective, one enters the system, accepts its internal postulates, and views the world from its standpoint. From the extrinsic perspective, the system itself becomes the object of perception and is viewed in the context of factors and influences external to it. The sociology of knowledge views intellectual phenomena in the formative social and historical setting of their origin and investigates the dependence of thought upon its social milieu. A close relationship can thus be seen between the historical-cultural relativity clarified by the studies in the sociology of knowledge, and the personal-subjective relativity with which the psychology of knowledge is concerned. Both disciplines apply an extrinsic perspective to intellectual activity, and both seek to define the dependence of knowledge upon its context. They differ only in the selection of the particular background factors against which they view ideas.

The powerful effects of subjective and personal factors on theory-building, it is apparent, coexist with equally powerful historical influences. A theory's language, its implicit and explicit postulates, even the empirical problems to which it addresses itself will all be conditioned by the period's prevailing paradigms and conceptual frameworks—which themselves are embedded in an encompassing scientific and philosophical weltanschauung and in still broader cultural and sociological processes. The dependence of psychological understanding on its intellectual and historical context can become an intriguing object of investigation in its own right (Levenson 1972, Buss 1975). The personalistic, psychological studies presented in this book, because they largely omit intellectual and historical contexts, can not therefore be construed as exhaustive accounts—nor are they meant to be.

The psychology and sociology of knowledge, which are in our view interdependent disciplines, must ultimately enter into a cooperative enterprise if the determinants of intellectual phenomena are to be fully comprehended and clarified. Although each field can make a certain degree of independent progress, their analyses are allied and complementary. A beginning partial synthesis is exemplified in the "psycho-historical" studies of Erikson (1958, 1969) and more recently of Mazlish (1975) and Lifton (1974).

In the context of our present analyses, every theory of personality can be shown to contain elements deriving not only from the theorist's personal world, but also from the external social field of ideas and concepts within which he lives and works. The pervasive extent to which the latter is the case led Mannheim to consider intellectual systems as social creations. But the social and intellectual context of an individual's work is never entirely homogeneous, and the specific ways in which it enters his theory reflects the operation of subjective factors. Carl Jung and Wilhelm Reich, for example, were both for many years immersed in Freudian thought, with its emphasis on libidinal energies and mental dynamics, and if psychoanalysis had not existed, their intellectual projects would surely have taken different forms. But the distinctive way in which each theorist assimilated and transformed the Freudian ideas, as will be seen in later chapters, bears an unmistakable subjective imprint. Jung, partially because of the dramatically polaristic organization of his own subjective world, reacted to the psychoanalytic theory by reconceptualizing the libido as a qualitatively neutral psychic energy flowing between various opposing poles in the personality, e.g., introversion-extraversion, conscious-unconscious, etc. Reich, under the sway of his own personal and tragic involvement with the problem of sexuality, reaffirmed the sexual nature of the libido, equated it with life energy in general, and made the study of its suppression the theme of his life work.

The individualized ways in which these two theorists reacted to Freudian psychoanalysis are prototypical of the general relations between the intellectual and his milieu. Any application of a purely sociological perspective compresses the differences between individual thinkers so as to demonstrate the effects of a common social and intellectual environment. Similarly, a purely psychological level of analysis neglects the link between the theorist and his milieu and even runs the risk of mistakenly attributing socially determined aspects of his thinking to personal factors located in his unique life history.

Decentering in the Genesis of Knowledge

This book is in the nature of a proposal concerning the future of personality psychology. Our thesis is that the continuing progress of the field will depend upon the clarification of limiting subjective influences in theory building and on the elaboration of concepts and methods belonging to a level of generality higher than that hitherto attained. We envision a beginning differentiation between the subjectivity of individual theories and the empirical phenomena they seek to explain, whereby the existent conflicts between various metapsychologies might be resolved. This differentiation between subject and object in the development of personality theory finds close analogues in the critical advances which occur in other disciplines.

Piaget, in *The Place of the Sciences of Man in the System of Sciences* (1970), offers the following useful formulation of the beginning phases of knowledge:

The two most ready tendencies of spontaneous thought, and even of speculation at its initial stages, are to assume that one stands at the center of the world, both spiritual and material, and to elevate one's own rules or even habits into universal standards [p. 13].

Accordingly, one of the essential features of an advance to the next stage of thought consists in a decentering process whereby an initial view is transcended by a more general standpoint. What had earlier been envisioned as universal and objective is now recognized as particular and subjective. A failure to recognize one's viewpoint as particularized amounts to a state of non-differentiation from the object world. The further construction of a more inclusive and decentered group of ideas resolves this non-differentiation. It gives rise to a two-fold deepening of knowledge, wherein a sharpened self-consciousness is accompanied by a more articulate perception of the structures of objective reality.

Such transformations of perspective are especially clearly illustrated in the revolutions of modern physics. The twentieth century has seen a development from the classical Newtonian intuition of the universe as an infinite, three-dimensional network subsisting in absolute homogeneous time to a four-dimensional space-time geometry in which various measurements of the physical world are shown to be a function of the frame of reference of the observer. In the theory of relativity, what had previously been taken for objective existence became only a special case in a system of equally valid alternative appearances. The theory of the world's structure thereby liberated itself from the concrete immediacy of human intuition and assumed the more general form of principles relating the different possible perspectives to one another. Similarly, quantum mechanics disclosed various features of the microscopic domain incompatible with classical concepts of objective motion, spatial localization, and causal interaction. These concepts were then recognized as no longer referring to anything ultimately objective, but rather to the appearance of reality from a now particularized macroscopic perspective and as limiting cases of more general quantum mechanical laws.

Piaget (1970) convincingly argues that the decentering—or subject-object differentiating—process characterizes not only the evolution of the physical sciences, but also the sciences of man. In sociology, for example, the line of development from Rousseau through Marx to Mannheim, and more recently to Gouldner (1970), is one in which social reality is understood less and less on the model of personal thought, and the individual (even including his sociological theories) is seen ever more clearly as the product of a social process. This gradual transformation implies not only a better understanding of society in its own terms, decentered from the subjective experience of the individual, but also a much clearer and differentiated self-awareness on the part of its observers. The existence of linguistics as a discipline also presupposes a rather profound decentering from the belief that one's language is intrinsically bound up in the fabric of reality (the natural view of young children), and a recognition of its status as only one among an indefinitely large number of possible symbol systems. The transition of linguistic science from its descriptive phase to the structuralist and transformational school would also seem to exemplify the principle of decentering. The developing knowledge of language at the level of its "deep structure" is formulated in principles of increasing abstractness and generality, and appears to be progressively separating itself from categories belonging to particular linguistic communities. The program outlined by Chomsky (1965) includes the clarification of universals underlying the empirical diversity of human languages, and promises to elucidate the nature of symbolic communication systems—and hence of the human perspective on the world—in a radically new way. The findings of cultural anthropology likewise show a deepened awareness of the link between experienced reality and milieu, and thus imply a decentering of thought from its embeddedness within a particular cultural and historical setting. One sees as well a process of self-object differentiation in the history of psychoanalysis. The growing appreciation of the psychology of individual patients was returned upon the analyst's understanding of himself, and the critical concept of countertransference was formulated. This recognition of the subjectivity of the analyst's experiences in the form of countertransference manifestations in turn established the possibility of a still deeper and more articulated knowledge of the analytic patient. The issues with which this book is concerned are closely allied with the psychoanalytic notion of the countertransference, for we interpret the metapsychological suppositions of the various theories as reflecting particularized countertransferential attitudes, to be superceded by a more general framework.

The study of the subjectivity of personality theory, although related to intellectual issues having a long history and cutting across many disciplines, is uniquely modern. It could not have been undertaken had competing, alternate systems not existed. Such a study includes comparative analysis and research, in which differing interpretations of a common set of phenomena are juxtaposed, and in which the principles relating them are established. These principles, if they are intended to contribute to the development of the field as a whole, should be formulated to transcend the personal limits embodied in the theories considered, and be capable of accounting for phenomena outside the theories' particularized ranges of applicability.

ATTEMPTED CIRCUMVENTIONS OF SUBJECTIVITY

Behaviorism

The importance of considering the subjective dimension of psychological knowledge (and of human behavior in general) is by no means universally recognized, and a number of approaches have evolved which directly or indirectly seek to circumvent the issues and problems we have been discussing. Perhaps the most radical of these appears in the school of thought known as behaviorism, where the whole concept of man as an experiencing subject is eliminated. In the history of psychological ideas behaviorism arose as a reaction to an excessive emphasis upon the analysis and description of consciousness, and especially to the insubstantial controversies of the introspectionist movement associated with Wundt and Titchener. Although it quickly ramified into a whole variety of subschools and individualized "theories of learning," all of its branches, practical and theoretical, share one common postulate; namely, that the discipline of psychology is a natural science and must be founded upon the primary and unassailable fact that man is an objective organism behaving in an objective physical and social environment. Efforts were made to expunge from the professional thinking of psychologists such concepts as "mind," "consciousness," "will," etc.; and these efforts left their imprint on the currently prevailing definition of the field as the *science of behavior*. Although behaviorism is no longer widely accepted as a theoretical foundation for psychology, an analysis of certain of its ideas and assumptions will assist us in further characterizing the essential inescapability of the problem of subjectivity. We shall focus in our discussion on the ideas of B.F. Skinner, for he is certainly the preeminent living exponent of behaviorism, and his influence on American psychology has been especially widespread.

Ever since psychology began to separate itself from philosophy during the nineteenth century, a great many of its schools have sought to model themselves on the image of the natural sciences. This holds true in particular for Skinnerian behaviorism. Skinner's *Science and Human Behavior* (1953) begins with some comments on what he regards as the important components of the natural scientific attitude, and then proceeds to argue that this attitude can be directed toward the "behavior of organisms" as a new domain of phenomena for investigation. His discussions make clear that he considers the elucidation of the causality of behavior as the essential task for a scientific psychology. This is indicated by the tenor of his criticisms of other approaches, in which he describes such supposedly causally efficacious entities as "inner need states," "intentions," and "the self" as pre-scientific, spurious pseudo-explanations which beg the question of the real factors determining human behavior. In *Beyond Freedom and Dignity* (1971), he asserts that in the same way the natural sciences made progress by de-animating and de-personifying nature, the progress of psychology will depend upon the de-animation and de-personification of man:

> We can follow the path taken by physics and biology by...neglecting the supposed mediating states of mind. Physics did not advance by looking more closely at the jubilance of falling bodies, or biology by looking at the nature

of vital spirits, and we do not need to try to discover what personalities, states of mind, feelings, traits of character, plans, purposes, intentions or the other perquisites of autonomous man *really are* in order to get on with a scientific analysis of behavior [p. 15].

The primacy of causality in Skinner's thought is also indicated by the system he offers as an alternative, wherein he places by far the greatest emphasis on the controlling reinforcement contingencies presumed to universally guide and regulate the course of human lives. To understand the determinants of behavior, one must ruthlessly discard the pre-scientific mentalism of past ages, shift the focus of study to the environment, and clarify the ways in which external variables shape and control the behavior of the individual.

Skinner's critique of doctrines which postulate the existence of internal mental agencies operating as irreducible sources of conduct strikes us as not entirely unfounded, for such doctrines tend to intermingle and confuse metapsychological and phenomenological levels of analysis. For example, the phenomenological *experience* of freedom and efficacy may be reified in the image of an internal but nevertheless objectified (and universalized) entity which is conceived to literally intervene in the causal nexus of events. But this is not quite Skinner's line of argument. He seems to believe that demonstrating the spuriousness of a reified concept is equivalent to disproving the existence of the experience from which it derives, as if subjective states could not exist except in thing-like (reified) form. Skinner conceptualizes phenomena ordinarily described in mentalistic terms as "private events" and "covert behavior," which are not directly accessible to others but are in all other respects analogous to the publicly observable behavior of the organism. He thereby transforms the "subjective world" of the individual into a covert but nonetheless objective set of events which, pending the invention of suitable physiological instrumentation, is knowable only through inference. Here we see the radically consistent, relentless objectivism of Skinnerian thought, in which the image of man as an experiencing subject is eliminated, and the phenomena previously relegated to the domain of consciousness are transposed into the sphere of "objective reality."

This transposition from consciousness to "objective reality" seems to us a highly dubious affair. As we said earlier, Skinner's various critiques of mentalism (1953, 1971, 1974) focus upon the use of mental and subjective concepts in explaining the causality of behavior. He argues, for example, against the notions of the self as "an originating agent within the organism" (1953, p. 283), against "emotions...as fictional causes to which we attribute behavior" (p. 160), and against inner need states, such as thirst or hunger, as invoking an "inner causal agent which cannot serve as an explanation" (p. 33). He is repeatedly saying that subjective phenomena are not objective, for causal efficacy is a property of objective events. But in his own alternative to mentalism, subjective experience becomes "covert behavior" and therefore turns out to be objective after all. It would appear that Skinner's system has simply substituted a new set of misleading reifications for the old ones. Even if the hypothesized "private" and "covert" behavioral processes could be shown to exist, perhaps amplified on the high-science instrumentation of the future, the most one could expect to observe would be *objective correlates*, and not, as he implies, the experiences themselves.

It might further be asked how the substance of the problem of the subjectivity of knowledge is dealt with by Skinnerian thought. His behaviorism, a radically consistent one, takes for granted that the investigative activity of the psychologist is under the control of the same kind of contingencies of reinforcement which are being studied. As a consequence, the pathway which the activity follows will be circumscribed and partially determined by the particularities of the investigator's own life history. One could thus in principle pursue the psychology of knowledge from an exclusively Skinnerian perspective and study the functional relationships between theoretical formulations and the reinforcement contingencies prevailing in the theorist's past and present environments. But such an enterprise, owing to the conceptual impoverishment of Skinner's approach, would in our view be doomed to failure. A theory of man, for example, could never be treated as reflecting a more or less coherent subjective vision of the world, emerging as a solution to developmental crises and dilemmas, but rather as a set of private and public behaviors which would have to be analyzed in a piecemeal fashion. It is difficult to imagine such a project providing anything more in the way of results than the notion that theorists formulate their theories in the ways they do because they have been reinforced for doing so. The major limitation of Skinnerian behaviorism as a workable foundation for the psychology of knowledge, and more generally for a science of human personality, lies in its lack of synthetic heuristic principles to guide the interpretation of psychological and life-historical phenomena. Skinner's system is metapsychologically atomistic and externalistic in orientation, envisioning human conduct universally as a set of empirically separable objective behaviors and tracing functional relationships in which the sources of causality are always finally located in the external world. This limiting focus is, of course, also the origin of its considerable power as a practical technology even to those who disagree with Skinner's speculative premises regarding human nature.

Methodological Objectivism

A position less extreme than that of behaviorism, but one which also exemplifies an attempted circumvention of the problem of subjectivity, is represented by the notion that the personal concerns of the investigator are potential contaminating influences and therefore pose dangers to the scientific value of his research. This position, which we shall call "methodological objectivism," is not so much a psychological theory as it is a philosophy of the relationship between the scientist and his work. It emphasizes a disjunction between the investigator as a person and the material he studies, and aims at establishing universally verifiable, purely objective truths, divorced from the human context in which they are discovered. The idealization of pure objectivity is here accompanied by a deprecation of any thinking which passes beyond established facts. It is also accompanied by a devaluation of the personal needs, wishes, and interests of the scientist, such factors being interpreted as "experimenter bias" to be controlled and eliminated. The aim of dissociating scientific research from the potential mistakenness of the scientist's speculative ideas and subjectivity then becomes translated into the particular methods of investigation and into "acceptable" criteria of evidence. These methods contain elaborate safeguards against the intrusion of various sources of error into the research, chief among them being the investigator's personal concerns and emotional investment in his ideas. Correspondingly, the criteria of evidence for assessing the plausibility of an interpretation are of an exceedingly stringent nature, tied closely to demonstrable (and preferably quantitative) empirical data.

From the perspective of "methodological objectivism," psycho-biographical and intensive case analysis would be construed as an especially dangerous and seductive procedure, for there is no safeguard against error other than the investigator's judgment, and opportunities for speculative and subjective distortion of the material are very great. On the other hand, let us consider for a moment the consequences for personality research of adopting an objectivist philosophy of method.

The consequences of the objectivist quest for freedom from error and personal bias involve a narrowing of the range of problems which can be studied and an alienation of the psychologist from his own research. Experimental methods replace correlational and descriptive ones, which are associated with an uncertainty of interpretation. But this drastically curtails the discipline's empirical field and sharply reduces the significance of the problems it can study; for phenomena of human personality (certainly theoretically interesting ones) which a practical experimental (or even correlational) paradigm can capture are few and far between. The exigencies of objectivist experimentation further require that the variables of interest be "operationalized," a procedure which more often than not in modern personality research introduces a profound degree of distortion and ambiguity into the issues being investigated. Ultimately the impact of these factors on the field as a whole produces an inversion of priorities, wherein the methods deemed acceptable begin to dictate the problems being studied rather than the other way about (see McGuire 1973). In addition, the protection against the supposedly contaminating influences of subjective bias is limited, for the personal concerns of the investigator will affect his selection of problems and variables to study, the specific empirical questions he poses, and his understanding of the implications of his final results.

While there is a conceptual disunity in the field of personality theory, there is an almost unrelieved "sprawl and diversity" in personality research (Adelson 1969). Personality research contends not only with metapsychological conflicts of various kinds, but also with the fragmenting and trivializing effects of prevailing objectivist opinion. The devaluation of speculative thought inhibits serious theorizing, diverts the attention of investigators from issues of broad human significance, and refocuses their research interests upon ever more narrowly defined and atheoretical problems. The pursuit of unassailable objectivity subordinates the task of discovery to the task of verification, and defers theory-building pending the establishment of reliable, demonstrable facts. Kelly characterized this trend of psychological research with the phrase, "accumulative fragmentalism."

> A scientist...who thinks this way, and especially a psychologist who does so, depends upon his facts to furnish the ultimate proof of his propositions. With these shining nuggets of truth in his grasp it seems unnecessary for him to take responsibility for the conclusions he claims they thrust upon him [Quoted in Bannister and Mair 1968, pp. 6–7].

A further consequence of objectivism is that it strips the issues of their human contexts and loses sight of its presumptively central concern with the experience and conduct of persons (Carlson 1971). The knowledge being elaborated thus deals less and less with human beings, and more and more with relationships between disembodied "personality variables," e.g., introversion and creativity, locus of control and persistence in tasks, etc.

The objectivist deprecation of personal bias and speculative thinking is itself an ideological and subjective stance, and one that is by no means shared by all scientists (e.g., the analysis of the personal dimension of scientific knowing by Polanyi 1958). Furthermore it intrudes upon the conduct of personality research, limiting its empirical domain, trivializing the problems it studies,

and excluding a quest for broader theoretical understanding. In a
recent review of the field Sechrest was led to an impression with
which we would agree.

> The individual studies lack direction...and they suggest a
> status for the field of personality that puts one in mind of the
> apocryphal jet pilot who assured his passengers that while the
> plane was lost, it was at least making good time [1976, p. 22].

Phenomenology

Let us now consider another system of thought which seeks an
escape from the problems and difficulties associated with the
subjectivity of psychological knowledge: so-called "pure phenomenology." Phenomenology arose historically from Cartesian and
Kantian philosophy and is a discipline which attempts to establish
itself as the descriptive science of the primordial phenomena of
human consciousness. Edmund Husserl, in his classic work *Ideas:
An Introduction to Pure Phenomenology* (1931), envisioned the
goal of this enterprise as the systematic characterization of
"transcendental subjectivity," i.e., of the invariant structures of
consciousness which constitute the ultimate conditions of the
possibility of all conscious experience. By virtue of its focus on the
preconditions of all conceivable experience, phenomenology was
regarded by Husserl as a field more basic than the specialized
developments of empirical consciousness represented by the
traditional sciences (including psychology).

Husserl proposed to investigate "transcendental subjectivity" by
means of a procedure which lies at the heart of his researches: *the
phenomenological reduction.* This entails a graded series of
alterations of perspective, beginning from a naturalistic standpoint
of consciousness of the world, passing reflexively through a phase
in which empirical consciousness itself (rather than empirical
reality) becomes the object of study, and eventuating in the
disclosure of the unanalyzable pure essence which invests the world
with its meaning and validity: the transcendental ego. The
successive steps in the phenomenological reduction are said to
correspond with various fields of science: the naturalistic

standpoint is the perspective underlying the natural sciences as investigations of objective reality; the reflexive phase in which the facts of consciousness come into view corresponds with "descriptive phenomenology" or "phenomenological psychology"; and the invariant essences which inhere in the concrete data of experience are the objects of study for "transcendental phenomenology."

One of the central components of the Husserlian reduction is called "bracketing": an intellectual operation through which the phenomenologist frees himself from preconceptions and achieves the purity of the transcendental perspective. "Bracketing," then, refers to a radical alteration of one's position in relation to all those assumptions, beliefs, and attitudes which in the natural standpoint are taken for granted; indeed, which constitute "the thesis of the natural standpoint" (p. 91). These include one's belief in the existence of objective reality, one's knowledge of the spatial and temporal arrangement of the world, even one's experience of oneself as a subjectivity associated with a physically delimited and localized body. The natural world as a system of empirical objects is "bracketed," all implicit and explicit assumptions concerning it are held in suspension, and the investigating consciousness is refocused upon the pure ("eidetic") essences of the concrete data of experience *per se.* Husserl does not argue for the elimination of external reality in the pursuit of transcendental discoveries, for all of one's experiences are retained; but they are retained in a different form than is the case under the ordinary conditions of perception. It is not the world which disappears in the phenomenological reduction, but rather the world-as-objective, which is to say the complex of presuppositions underlying its manifestations to naturalistic consciousness. The operation of bracketing objective reality also transforms the mode in which consciousness appears in reflection to itself:

If we now perform the transcendental-phenomenological reduction, the psychological subjectivity loses just that which makes it something real in the world that lies before us; it loses the meaning of the soul as belonging to a body that exists in an objective spatio-temporal Nature [p. 8].

The principal value of the Husserlian quest for a presupposition-free science of experience is as a critique of the unclarified and unfounded metaphysical assumptions embedded in Lockean empiricism (and in all of its philosophical and psychological derivatives): an implicit mind-body dualism; an image of consciousness as a quasi-spatial container; a view of man as the passive receptor of discrete, elementary sensations from the world. The capacity of phenomenology to pass beyond the status of a critique and to literally fulfill its stated aims of elucidating transcendental subjectivity, however, seems to us fraught with difficulties. To discover and describe the ultimate preconditions of all conscious experience would require an observer who stands entirely outside of the human domain, whose perceptions and intuitions are not conditioned by the structures he contemplates and (since these structures are posited as ultimates) whose observations are not conditioned by anything whatsoever. In short, it would require a transcendental consciousness of truly god-like proportions. Secondly, in regard to the "bracketing" of objective reality in the phenomenological reduction (which even divests subjectivity of its physical embodiment), what is to guarantee that this operation does not transform the data of conscious experience so as to make the description of "eidetic essences" spurious? Furthermore, can this suspension of belief in objective existence be carried out without becoming involved in a contradiction? For what of all those unsuspended presuppositions embedded in the intention to conduct this research which surely include the prospect of communicating results and of contributing to human knowledge? The research attitude, in other words, would seem inevitably to reinsert the assumptive basis of the phenome-nologist's activities into the spatio-temporal world.

Still another problem implicit in the concept of "bracketing" pertains to the cumulative effects of the phenomenologist's life history. Such inescapable (non-bracketable) influences pose a danger to the "purity" of his investigations, limiting their generality and validity. Furthermore, Husserl's intention to explore transcendental subjectivity did not spring into existence *de novo*, nor is it by any means an inevitable reaction to the traditions of intellectual history (witness the diversity of philosophical positions); it represents, in part, a particular personal and subjective stance in relation to those traditions, embodying within its own structure the impact of a life-historical process whose "objectivity" it ostensibly suspends.

The Husserlian program to describe transcendental subjectivity is accompanied by an implicit goal of stepping outside the bounds of personal existence into an unconditioned realm of pure objectivity on pure subjectivity. This we regard as an impossible feat, except as an imaginary infinite limit toward which psychological knowledge may be conceived to be evolving. In addition, the emphasis in phenomenology on establishing a descriptive science free of presuppositions, its tendency to always start over again with the uncontaminated facts of experience, rules out any genuine advance in its discoveries; for the essence of the accumulation of scientific knowledge lies in the testing, reformulating, and deepening of presuppositions regarding the material under study.

The methods and concepts of phenomenology have penetrated psychology and have even led to attempts to refound the field on an existential-phenomenological basis (e.g., Sartre 1953, Binswanger 1963, Van Kaam 1969). These attempts, which in greater or lesser degree share Husserl's idealization of assumption-free description, have been of considerable value in criticizing and clarifying preconceptions in various domains of psychological inquiry (e.g., perception, imagination, and emotion). However, they are of circumscribed usefulness in the evolution of psychological knowledge, which depends upon formulation of assumptions and presuppositions regarding human experience and conduct, and on the testing of those assumptions against empirical human phenomena.

THE CASE STUDY METHOD

The chapters which follow (2–5) are psychobiographical in their approach and illustrate the method known as the intensive, indepth case study (Murray 1938, White 1952, 1963). This method has a long and distinguished history, being the principal approach taken by the major analytic theorists. Three general features distinguish it from other methodological orientations. First, it is inherently *personalistic* and *phenomenological.* It presupposes that the issues being investigated in personality research can be fully understood only if viewed in the context of the individual's personal world. Second, it is *historical*; the personal world is recognized as a life-historical phenomenon so that the issues of research are located on the temporal dimension of personal development. These two features already remove this method from the mainstream of academic personality research, wherein it is traditional to strip the variables under study of their phenomenological-historical contexts (which then become sources of random error) and investigate them across a population of different individuals. The third distinguishing feature of the case study approach is that it is *clinical* and *interpretive* (rather than experimental or deductive). It advances the understanding of individuals not by the testing of delimited hypotheses arrived at on some independent basis, but through a process of interrogation and construction evolved from the empirical materials at hand. Repeatedly it raises the interpretive question of what the experiential and life-historical context is within which various regions of the person's behavior have meaning. Eventually it arrives at a system of provisional constructions founded on the interpretation of the different parts of the case material, and cross-links and cross-validates these constructions, so that the plausibility of particular insights and hypotheses concerning the person can be assessed against the combined weight of the case analysis.

Psychobiographical analysis is an empirical procedure that always entails a complex back-and-forth movement between theoretical constructions and the phenomena being studied. The validity of its final formulations is nevertheless not easily assessed by any simple empirical method. It's overall validity can only be tentatively established, and it relies upon relatively subjective criteria pertaining to coherence of argument, comprehensiveness of explanation, and consistency with accepted psychological knowledge. For this reason most research psychologists have abandoned such analysis as a tool of inquiry in favor of the more "certain" results presumed to be available in the academic laboratory. This abandonment is in our view based on a deplorably mistaken understanding of the purposes and rationale of the case-study approach, the goal of which is not to arrive at final truths and incontrovertible general principles, but rather at significant theoretical ideas and promising lines of research. This approach is primarily a strategy of discovery and not a strategy of proof (Smith, Bruner and White 1956).

In an earlier section of this chapter we argued that the psychobiographical analysis of systems of personality theory must be founded upon a viewpoint more general than the specific theories being analyzed. Let us briefly consider the consequences of studying and tracing the personal origin of a theory while remaining strictly within its own domain of concepts and terms. This would entail applying the ideas of a personality theory to explain and account for those very ideas—a procedure of questionable value. With respect to that critical construct in psychoanalysis, the Oedipus complex, for example, such an analysis would merely seek to disclose the psychological and life-historical circumstances in which Freud's oedipal struggle emerged from repression into consciousness. It could not shed light on *why* Freud experienced it as a nuclear crisis of development, or *why* he attributed to it such crucial human significance, for the universality of the Oedipus complex is presupposed in Freudian theory. Or in the case of Jung, consider the problem of accounting for his early experience of being literally two persons (his No. 1 and No. 2 personalities) strictly within the framework of analytical psychology. One could only say he was precociously sensitized to the polarized tension between conscious and unconscious regions of the psyche, because the essential conflict embodied in this two-fold personification of himself is posited by Jungian theory as endemic to human nature. For Wilhelm Reich, the tragic suicide of his mother could not be seen as organically related to, or responsible for, his theory of man, but would at most be viewed as a mere predisposing factor underlying his discovery of the worldwide historical destructive power of sexual repression. Likewise, the strivings for self-immortalization and self-glorification which so color and pervade Rank's history of personal experiences would be interpreted within his system as simply an especially clear manifestation of the universal human will. In other words, the psychological analysis of personality theorists from within their own systems inevitably loses sight of their finiteness and personal limitations, and casts them as existential heroes who, almost miraculously it seems, uncovered the fundamental structures and motivations which universally determine the human condition.

What then is to be the theoretical foundation of our own psychobiographical analyses? We are in the paradoxical position of requiring a more embracing standpoint from which earlier theories can be shown to be limited and particularized, without having such a system explicitly worked out. Indeed, this fact might foredoom our studies to failure. But two considerations mitigate against such a conclusion. First, we shall be drawing upon the accumulated knowledge of many different schools of thought, and especially upon their clinical and personological (as opposed to metapsychological) principles. A very extensive body of concrete knowledge concerning persons is available today, the disunity and fragmentation of the field of personality psychology being largely an artifact of the incompatible metapsychologies of its various systems. Second, our method of approach is intensive psychobiographical case analysis, a procedure sufficiently flexible to permit new theoretical ideas to be formulated and genuine psychological discoveries to be made. We shall thus be turning the method of investigation out of which the analytic theories originally developed back upon the theories themselves, and use our studies as explorations of the possibility of a more general framework.

The Representational World

In the psychobiographical analyses which follow, we have chosen as our focus the "representational world" (Sandler and Rosenblatt 1962), i.e., the organized array of representations and associated affects which pervade the person's subjective experiences. This representational world is to be distinguished from conscious experience, for it refers to the patterning (structuralization) of consciousness, to the sequences of representational configurations which experience persistently assumes (and avoids assuming), and to the network of conceptual, symbolic, and emotional meanings discernible in the flux of unreflecting subjectivity. The representational world bears a close kinship to the formulations of the child's world in the developmental psychology of Piaget (1937), to the system of personal constructs envisioned in the work of Kelly (1955), and to Binswanger's (1946) existential-phenomenological notion of "the world-design." It is the structure of a person's subjective world as disclosed by an intensive investigation of the repetitive themes and leitmotifs which dominate his life. The representational world constitutes a kind of pre-reflective background into which the events of the person's life are continuously assimilated and on the dimensions of which his experiences continuously take form.

In our case-study, psychobiographical research, the first phase consists of a provisional descriptive characterization of the individual's representational world. This means discovering and formulating the unique dimensions on which his experiences are organized, the central concerns and dilemmas which are for him subjectively salient, and the recurrent thematic configurations of self- and object-representations (and associated affects) which pervade his world. We do not presuppose specific content-variables in this empirical study of persons; for example, we do not assume that introversion-extraversion, autonomy-dependence, or any other analogous experiential dimension is critical to all subjective worlds. We presuppose, on the contrary, that the central organizing concerns of personality vary from one individual to another, and we therefore seek to determine and formulate these concerns on a personalized, case-by-case basis. In this respect, our method is an inherently idiographic phenomenological one sharply distinguished from all theoretical and research positions which study particular content-variables with an *a priori* assumption that these are meaningful (though perhaps in varying degrees) to everyone. Our phenomenological emphasis however is not a "pure" one by any means. That we suspend assumptions regarding the "universal content" of human experience, and "bracket" metapsychological principles in particular, does not mean that we presuppose nothing whatsoever. We assume that subjective experience, viewed across a variety of situations and over a sufficient span of time, is always thematically organized around some more or less coherent set of nuclear concerns and, furthermore, that these concerns arise out of critical formative events in a person's life. This supposition leads us to the second phase of our case studies—namely, to the clarification of the developmental origins and of the functional significance of the particular organizing configurations in the person's subjective representational world. We now view the provisionally identified pervading concerns and recurring themes of the person's life as embedded in the history of his psychological development. These formulations of the structure of his experience we juxtapose to information regarding his personal history, and there we reconstruct the genesis of his representational world. Obviously this second, genetic phase is not independent of the first. Our understanding of the person's present experiential states will to some extent guide our inquiry into his developmental history, and it will influence the determination of which formative events we should regard as critical. Conversely, information about critical developmental situations may alter and transform the provisional characterization of a representational world. Case studies thus become a dialectical process in which descriptive and genetic phases reciprocally interpenetrate and illuminate one another.

In our analyses (chapters 2–5) we view four metapsychological systems of personality theory as reflections of their creators' subjective representational worlds. We analyze each theory to disclose the distinctive configurations of self- and object-representations (and their associated affects), reified and universalized in the theory's conception of human nature and the human condition. Furthermore, we elucidate the developmental origins and functional significance of these configurations in the context of each theorist's formative life experiences and of his life's recurrent themes. In our concluding chapter, we discuss the implications of our psychobiographical analyses for a critique of metapsychology and for the construction of a more general framework to guide the study of human personality.

REFERENCES

Adelson, J. (1969). Personality. *Annual Review of Psychology* 20:217-252.

Atwood, G., and Tomkins, S. (1976). On the subjectivity of personality theory. *Journal of the History of the Behavioral Sciences* 12:166-177.

Bannister, D., and Mair, J. (1968). *The Evaluation of Personal Constructs.* New York: Academic Press.

Binswanger, L. (1963). *Being-in-the-World.* New York: Basic Books.

Buss, A. (1975). The emerging field of the sociology of psychological knowledge. *American Psychologist* 30:988-1002.

Carlson, R. (1971). Where is the person in personality research? *Psychological Bulletin* 75:203-219.

Chomsky, N. (1965). *Aspects of the Theory of Syntax.* Cambridge: M.I.T. Press.

Coan, R. (1973). Toward a psychological interpretation of psychology. *Journal of the History of the Behavioral Sciences* 9:313-327.

Erikson, E. (1958). *Young Man Luther.* New York: W.W. Norton.

———(1969). *Gandhi's Truth.* New York: W.W. Norton.

Gouldner, A. (1970). *The Coming Crisis of Western Sociology.* New York: Basic Books.

Husserl, E. (1931). *Ideas: An Introduction to Pure Phenomenology.* New York: Macmillan.

Jung, C. (1968). *Analytical Psychology: Its Theory and Practice.* New York: Pantheon.

Kelly, G. (1963). *A Theory of Personality.* New York: W.W. Norton.

Levenson, E. (1972). *The Fallacy of Understanding.* New York: Basic Books.

Lifton, R., ed. (1974). *Explorations in Psychohistory.* New York: Simon and Schuster.

Mannheim, K. (1936). *Ideology and Utopia.* New York: Harcourt Brace and World.

———(1952). The problem of a sociology of knowledge. In *Essays on the Sociology of Knowledge,* pp. 134-190. New York: Oxford University Press.

Mazlish, B. (1975). *James and John Stuart Mill.* New York: Basic Books.

McGuire, W. (1973). The yin and yang of progress in social psychology. *Journal of Personality and Social Psychology* 26:446-456.

Murray, H. (1938). *Explorations in Personality.* New York: Science Editions, 1962.

Piaget, J. (1937). *The Construction of Reality in the Child.* New York: Basic Books.

———(1970). *The Place of the Sciences of Man in the System of Sciences.* New York: Harper and Row.

Polanyi, M. (1958). *Personal Knowledge.* New York: Harper and Row.

Sandler, J., and Rosenblatt, B. (1962). The concept of the representational world. *Psychoanalytic Study of the Child* 17:128-145.

Sartre, J.P. (1953). *Existential Psychoanalysis.* Chicago: Henry Regnery.

Sechrist, L. (1976). Personality. *Annual Review of Psychology* 27:1-28.

Skinner, B. (1953). *Science and Human Behavior.* New York: Macmillan.

———(1971). *Beyond Freedom and Dignity.* New York: Alfred A. Knopf.

———(1974). *About Behaviorism.* New York: Alfred A. Knopf.

Smith, M., Brunner, J., and White, R. (1956). *Opinions and Personality.* New York: John Wiley.

Tomkins, S. (1965). Affect and the psychology of knowledge. In *Affect, Cognition, and Personality,* ed. S. Tomkins and C. Izard, pp. 72-97. New York: Springer.

Van Kaam, A. (1969). *Existential Foundations of Psychology.* New York.: Image Books.

White, R. (1952). *Lives in Progress.* New York: Holt, Rinehart and Winston.

———(1963). *The Study of Lives.* New York: Holt, Rinehart and Winston.

CHAPTER 2

Sigmund Freud

In view of Freud's great productivity, as well as the many shifts and alterations in his theoretical positions in the course of his creative years, a comprehensive psychobiographical analysis of his theoretical system would pose a task of staggering complexity and monumental proportions. Therefore, we have chosen to limit our study of Freud to an elucidation of the subjective sources in his life of certain features of his theory of psychosexual development. This theory, along with its metapsychological reifications pertaining to instinctual drives and drive energies, remained pivotal in Freud's thinking despite the radical changes which he made in a number of his other theoretical ideas. Because this theory remained pivotal, we assume an especially close connection between it and equally enduring subjective concerns which dominated his life history.

To the student of the subjectivity of personality theory, the Freudian system is of special interest because Freud's theories were so intimately tied to his self-analysis. In our view, any self-analysis is limited and circumscribed by the absence of a systematic transference analysis and by the fact that no individual can successfully stand completely outside of his own deepest conflicts and defenses. Our study focuses on aspects of Freud's early experiences and personality structure which were omitted from his self-analysis, but which nevertheless expressed themselves in the structure of his theoretical ideas. In particular, we shall argue that his theory of psychosexual development and its central metapsychological reifications may be partially viewed as serving a defensive-restitutive effort by Freud to protect an idealized image of his mother against profound unconscious ambivalence.

Our analysis is organized into three parts. In the first, we discuss Freud's early childhood experiences with a view toward reconstructing the critical formative influences on the development of his personality. In the second, we trace the impact of these experiences on the pattern of his intimate relationships as an adult. And in the third, we present an analysis of the theory of psychosexual development and of certain other features of the psychoanalytic system in the light of the subjective concerns which dominated Freud's personal existence.

AMBIVALENCE IN FREUD'S LIFE

Sigmund Freud was his mother's first-born child and her indisputable favorite: "A man who has been the indisputable favorite of his mother keeps for life the feeling of a conqueror, that confidence of success which often induces real success," he wrote later (Jones 1953, p.5). He was born in a caul, an event which was believed to signify future fame and happiness. Reinforced by the prophecy of an old woman in a pastry shop, his mother proudly believed she had brought a great man into the world (Jones 1953). Jones remarks on her later habit of referring to him as "*mein goldener Sigi*" p. 3). Freud's conscious attitudes toward her were lastingly positive, and they are vividly reflected in his characterization of the tie between mother and son as "altogether the most perfect, the most free from ambivalence of all human relationships" (1933 [1932], p. 133).

But as we shall argue, the positive, ambivalence-free quality of

Freud's conscious attitudes toward his mother was the product of a defensive idealization process that served to protect his image of their relationship from invasion by negative affects. We shall show also that this defensive idealization functioned ultimately to avert the dreaded emergence of murderous hostility toward her and to ward off the catastrophic possibility of object loss. In this first section we attempt to uncover the sources of Freud's need to idealize his mother in the events and circumstances of his early childhood.

Earliest Experiences

Freud was born in 1856 in Freiburg, Moravia, where he spent the first three years of his life. His family circle included his father, his mother, and an older half-brother, Philipp. Another half-brother, Emanuel, was married and lived nearby. Emanuel's son John was to become Freud's first playmate. There was also an old nurse in the household who took care of him until he was two and one half years old.

So far as is known, Freud enjoyed a positive and relatively undisturbed relationship with his mother during the first months of his infancy. In light of the great pride with which she received him into the world, it seems likely that this early period involved an unusually intense narcissistic symbiosis. When he was eleven months old, however, this early narcissistic bliss in which he was the sole recipient of her adoring care was shattered by the birth of a younger brother, Julius. Freud reacted to the intruder's appearance with jealousy and rage. Some eight months later, the brother died. He describes the impact of this (reconstructed through self-analysis) in a letter to Fliess:

> I greeted my brother (who was a year my junior and died after a few months) with ill wishes and genuine childish jealousy...his death left the germ of self-reproaches in me [1950 (1892–1899), p. 262.

He was nineteen months old at the time of Julius's death. The "germ of self-reproaches" suggests that Freud drew a cause-and-effect connection between his own jealous ill wishes and the brother's "disappearance." A natural childish belief in the magical potency of hostile feelings thereby received a powerful reinforcement. (See Schur 1972, pp. 153–171 for a detailed discussion of Freud's "non-vixit" dream and the significance in his life of death wishes and of the theme of "the guilt of the survivor.")

In addition to stimulating jealousy and resentment at the intruder, the arrival of a younger sibling would also be experienced as a betrayal by the mother and therefore as an infuriating disappointment in her. Significantly, Freud's discussions of his self-analysis mention no such reactions. The only references to his mother during these early years are exclusively positive, picturing her as an object of his sexual feelings and his love.

The reconstructions of the relationship between himself and the old nurse, on the other hand, are marked by an intense emotional ambivalence. In the same letter to Fliess, Freud describes this woman as "'the prime originator' (of my troubles)...ugly, elderly, but clever [and] who told me a great deal about God Almighty and Hell..." (p. 261). She chided him for being incompetent and clumsy, encouraged him to steal money for her, and generally gave him "bad treatment" (p. 263). The experiential contrast between the nurse and the early image of his mother is striking. Through displacement, we believe, the nurse is pictured as bad and is held responsible for his neurotic suffering, while the mother is, by implication, absolved, and is preserved as an idealized object.

The ties to the old nurse, however, also had many positive elements. Freud states that she gave him a high opinion of his own capacities, provided him with the means of living and surviving at an early age, and comments to Fliess about how, in the midst of his complaints against her, his "old liking breaks through again" (p. 262). The nurse was Catholic and took him with her to church. When they returned home from church, the very young Freud would preach sermons to his parents and tell them all about how God conducted his affairs. This was during the middle of Freud's third year, a time when his mother had again become less available owing to the impending birth of another child, this time his sister, Anna. One gains the impression that the nurse functioned as a surrogate mother and provided young Freud with a continuity of care during those periods when his mother was occupied with bearing children.

The events surrounding Anna's birth were critically important ones for the development of Freud's personality, we believe, for not only did another infuriating rival for his mother's love appear, but the nurse herself now suddenly vanished from his life. Philipp, the older half-brother, discovered that she had been stealing during the mother's confinement and the nurse was arrested and imprisoned. The disappearance of his nurse, as we see by the following description and analysis, must have been a shattering and incomprehensible trauma for Freud, and he must have become intensely frightened of a similar "disappearance" of his mother. He describes to Fliess the impact of this trauma in the context of interpreting an obscure early memory:

> I said to myself that if the old woman disappeared so suddenly, it must be possible to point to the impression this made on me.... A scene then occurred to me which, for the last 29 years, has occasionally emerged in my conscious memory without my understanding it. My mother was nowhere to be found: I was screaming my head off. My brother Philipp, twenty years older than me, was holding open a cupboard for me, and when I found that my mother was not inside it either, I began crying still more, till, looking slim and beautiful, she came in by the door [p. 264].

In analyzing the memory, Freud tried to understand why he should have imagined that his mother had been locked inside a cupboard (*Kasten*). According to his reconstruction, he had asked Philipp what had happened to the nurse, and had received the answer, "She has been locked up" (*Sie ist eingekastelt*). But his young mind interpreted this to mean she had been locked in a cupboard, and so when he later (in the "scene") missed his mother, he became terrified that she had been disposed of in the same way. Interestingly, his later "phobia" of traveling by train was seen by Jones (1953) to be a derivative of his fear of losing his home and ultimately his mother's breast.

Freud's attitudes toward the nurse included, as we have seen, powerful hostile feelings; indeed, he later envisioned her bad treatment of him as the prime cause of his psychological difficulties. Insofar as these negative feelings were already manifest while she was still an active part of his life, there must have been many occasions when he wished her gone so that he would be released from her oppressive and bad treatment. Her sudden disappearance, therefore, must have been experienced like the earlier disappearance of Julius—as a magical fulfillment of his ill wishes. His sense of the omnipotence of his hostile feelings was thus again dramatically reinforced. But the vanishing of the nurse did not mean simply an escape from something wholly bad; it was also a security-shattering loss of all those elements in their relationship which he had loved and needed.

We are now in a position to interpret the nature of Freud's subsequent fear of losing his mother and also of his defensive need to preserve an entirely positive and idealized image of her. The intense separation anxiety presented in the early memory concerned a fear that his mother had fallen victim to the terrible fate of the nurse; i.e., its unconscious meaning is that the mother was in danger of being similarly shut away from the world and annihilated by Freud's own omnipotent hostile feelings toward her. We believe that the primary source of his hostility in this connection was that his mother had once again betrayed his love by bringing another hateful intruder into the world (five additional siblings were born in subsequent years).[1] The central conflict in his emotional life had thus been established; namely, the conflict between an intense, possessive need for his mother's love and an equally intense, magically potent hatred. By splitting off, repressing, and displacing the enraging and disappointing qualities of the mother image, he safeguarded his relationship to her from invasion by negative affects, protected her from the overwhelming power of his anger, and saved himself from the dreaded catastrophe of losing her.

The contrast between Freud's images of his early tie to his mother and his reconstructions of the other significant relationships of his early childhood is extreme and striking. We have already seen that his nurse was the object of ambivalent feelings. A combination of love and hate was likewise present in his early attitudes toward his father, although this was only clarified in his self-analysis with the discovery of his own Oedipus complex, *after* his father had already died. Freud's relationship to his nephew John was also characterized by the coexistence of strong positive and negative feelings; indeed, his self-analytic reconstructions picture John as friend and enemy similtaneously (1900, p. 483). In the midst of the strife-ridden love-hate entanglements of Freud's early years, the singular image of the exclusively positive tie to the mother stands out as a defensively encapsulated island of uncontaminated security and love.

Freud's struggles against feelings of hatred toward his mother are interestingly reflected in a section of *The Interpretation of Dreams* (1900) devoted to a discussion of anxiety dreams:

> It is dozens of years since I myself had a true anxiety dream. But I remember one from my seventh or eighth year, which I submitted to interpretation some thirty years later. It was a very vivid one, and in it I saw my beloved mother, with a peculiarly peaceful, sleeping expression on her features, being carried into the room by two (or three) people with birds' beaks and laid upon the bed. I awoke in tears and screaming, and interrupted my parents' sleep [p. 583].

His associations to the dream included the ideas that the bird-beaked figures were drawn from an Egyptian funerary relief and that the peaceful expression on his mother's face was copied from the view he had had of his comatose grandfather a few days before his death. Hence, the images implied that she was dead or dying.

> I awoke in anxiety, which did not cease till I had woken my parents up. I remember that I suddenly grew calm when I saw my mother's face, as though I needed to be reassured that she was not dead [pp. 583–584].

This childhood dream contains, we believe, a vivid and almost undisguised fulfillment of Freud's hostile death wishes toward his mother. Such an interpretation is supported by an earlier section of the book entitled, "Dreams of the Death of Persons of Whom the Dreamer Is Fond," wherein Freud distinguishes two classes of these dreams: those in which the dreamer is emotionally unaffected, and those in which he feels deeply pained by the death. The first of these classes, he argues, have some meaning other than the apparent one and conceal in their latent content some other wish. But of the second class he writes:

> Very different are the dreams of the other class—those in which the dreamer imagines the death of a loved relative and is at the same time painfully affected. The meaning of such dreams, as their content indicates, is a wish that the person in question may die [p. 249].

Clearly, Freud's emotionally overwhelming dream of his mother's dying belongs to this second class. But in his own discussion of the dream, he retreats from such an interpretation and is at pains to show that the image of the dying mother is not a fulfillment of his aggressive wishes; rather, he interprets it as an artifact of the dreamwork and as concealing deeper, sexual wishes. Here we have concrete evidence of the way in which Freud excluded hostile feelings from his recollections of his relationship with his mother, which remained in his memory exclusively affectionate and erotic.

ADULT RELATIONSHIPS

The two most important relationships of Freud's young and middle adulthood were dominated by his wish to restore and preserve the lost ideal union with his mother, which had been so traumatically disrupted by the births of Julius and Anna. These were with his wife Martha and with his mentor Wilhelm Fliess. First, however, we note that even Freud's decision to study medicine was strongly colored by this same need. In his own account:

> it was hearing Goethe's beautiful essay on Nature read aloud at a popular lecture...just before I left school that decided me to become a medical student [1925 [1924], p. 8].

This Jones (1953) enlarges:

> Goethe's dithyrambic essay is a romantic picture of Nature as
> a *beautiful and bountiful mother who allows her favorite
> children the privilege of exploring her secrets.* This imagery
> attracted the youthful Freud [p. 29. Italics added].

Freud's attraction to the study of Nature as a "beautiful and
bountiful mother" was the heir to his youthful longings to return to
his birthplace in the country where he had spent the happy times of
his early childhood (Jones 1953), which in turn, we believe,
expressed his wish to find again the lost paradise of his earliest tie
with his mother.

In another context Freud attributed his interest in medical
studies to the vicissitudes of his "infantile curiosity" and his
"overpowering need to understand something of the riddles of the
world in which we live..." (1927, p. 253). The unraveling of riddles
was to become the leitmotif of Freud's work. The first and most
decisive riddle in his life was his unfathomable mother, who
showered him with adoration and then betrayed him. Indeed,
women, as heirs to the riddle of the mother, seemed to remain for
Freud a great mystery:

> [The erotic life] of women...is still veiled in an impenetrable
> obscurity [1905, p. 151.].

> The great question that has never been answered and which I
> have not yet been able to answer, despite my thirty years of
> research into the feminine soul, is "What does a woman
> want?" [Jones 1955, p. 421].

Erikson (1954) has suggested that Freud eventually transferred
onto the dream the image of the mystifying, enchanting mother
whose deep secrets he wished to unveil.

If Freud hoped to refind his early idyllic tie to his mother in his
relationship to nature and to dreams, this was even more true of his
courtship of Martha Bernays. Jones (1953) describes Freud's

attitude toward his loved one as a *"grande passion"* (p. 109), and documents this characterization with ample quotations from the more than 900 letters Freud wrote to his betrothed during the four and a quarter years of their engagement (during which they were separated for three years). The nature and strength of Freud's idealizing needs are revealed in his early love letters:

> What I meant to convey was how much the magic of your being expresses itself in your countenance and your body, how much there is visible in your appearance that reveals how sweet, generous, and reasonable you are....Once the smoothness and freshness of youth is gone then the only beauty lies where goodness and understanding transfigure the features, and that is where you excel....In your face it is the pure noble beauty of your brow and your eyes that shows in almost every picture [Jones, 1953, p. 102].

According to Jones (1953),"[Freud's] first compliment...was to liken her to the fairy princess from whose lips fell roses and pearls, with, however, the doubt whether kindness or good sense came more often from Martha's lips" (p. 103).

During their prolonged separation Freud frequently experienced "a frightful yearning...an indescribable longing" to be reunited, so that all his troubles would vanish "as with a stroke of magic" (pp. 169–170). We can sense the awe and ecstasy and passion that Freud experienced in relation to the woman who was his "whole world" (p. 183), his "ideal of womanhood" (p. 176), the embodiment of total goodness, understanding, kindness and nobility.

In his voluminous letters to his idealized love object he chronicled in detail his hopes, struggles, and accomplishments. For instance, after winning a traveling grant to study with Charcot in Paris, he wrote to Martha exuberantly:

> Oh, how wonderful it is going to be. I am coming with money and am staying a long while with you and am bringing something lovely for you and shall then go to Paris and

become a great *savant* and return to Vienna with a great, great
nimbus. Then we shall marry soon and I will cure all the
incurable nervous patients and you will keep me well and I will
kiss you till you are merry and happy—and they lived happily
ever after [Jones, 1953, p. 76].

Clearly, he was attempting to revive with Martha his earliest idyllic
period when he experienced himself as the exclusive focus of his
mother's interest and adoration. It is equally noteworthy, however,
that throughout the engagement period he was excessively
preoccupied with Martha's health. The spectre of repressed
hostility emerged here in much the same manner that it did in his
early crisis of separation anxiety in relation to his mother. As was
undoubtedly the case with his mother, the loss of Martha "would
be absolutely equivalent to the end of the world" (p. 132).

Jones alludes to the difficulties which faced Freud when
Martha's real qualities proved recalcitrant to his intense need to
idealize her:

Freud's characteristic aversion to compromises...displayed
itself to the full in this greatest emotional experience of his life.
Their relationship must be quite perfect; the slightest blur was
not to be tolerated. At times it seemed as if his goal was fusion
rather than union. This aim...was bound to encounter
thwartings when confronted with a steadfast personality,
since Martha, with all her sweetness, was not a pattern of
yielding docility. Only a week after the parting there was the
first faint hint of his intention, never to be fulfilled, to mold
her into his perfect image [1953, p. 110].

Freud's wish to mold Martha into his "perfect image" was
intimately connected with his intense jealousy and possessiveness.
Shortly after their engagement, Freud displayed a jealous outburst
in relation to Martha's former suitor, Max Meyer. Afterwards he
wrote to her self-reproachfully:

Can there be anything crazier, I said to myself. You have won
the dearest girl quite without any merit of your own, and you

know no better than only a week later to reproach her with being tart and to torment her with jealousy. *The loved one is not to become a toy doll* but a good comrade who still has a sensible word left when the strict master has come to the end of his wisdom [Jones, 1953, pp. 110–111; italics added].

In connection with another rival, Fritz Wahle, whose affections Martha had encouraged while she was engaged to Freud, Freud wrote to her:

When the memory of your letter to Fritz... comes back to me I lose all control of myself, and had I the *power to destroy the whole world*... I would do so without hesitation [Jones 1953, pp. 114–115; italics added].

Could this passage reflect the revival of his unconscious and omnipotently destructive rage at his mother for betraying him in favor of his early rivals, Julius and Anna? Freud displayed a similarly violent fury whenever Martha failed to take his side in the antagonisms which later developed between him and Martha's brother and mother. He acknowledged a "talent for interpreting" (Jones 1953, p. 17) between the lines of Martha's letters and finding evidence of her disloyalty to him. According to Jones, Freud required from Martha:

...complete identification with himself, his opinions, his feelings and his intentions. She was not really his unless he could perceive his 'stamp' on her.... Possessiveness, exclusiveness in affection, absolute fusion of attitudes towards various people...... The demand that gave rise to the most trouble was that she should not simply be able to criticize her mother and brother... but she had also to withdraw all affection from them—this on the grounds that they were his enemies, so that she should share his hatred of them. If she did not do this she did not really love him [p. 122–123].

We believe that Freud's need to mold Martha into an idealized image of perfection, a mother-surrogate who loved him exclusively, with total loyalty and devotion, stemmed from his unconscious desire to prevent a repetition of the traumatic betrayals he had experienced with his actual mother. Most importantly, he sought to ward off the dreaded emergence of the split-off image of the hated mother and of his own repressed, omnipotently destructive rage at her. Freud's reactions to disappointments by Martha are most enlightening. His jealous outbursts were more often than not followed by self-reproaches, which can be understood as serving his need to restore the intactness of Martha's (i.e., his mother's) perfect image. This dynamic was also in evidence when, near the end of their engagement, Martha revealed that she had become aware of some "bad thoughts" within herself. Freud's reaction was telling:

> I had believed you didn't know such things. There are people who are good because nothing evil occurs to them, and others who are good because they conquer their evil thoughts. I had reckoned you to the former class. *No doubt it is my fault* that you have lost your guilelessness [Jones, p. 125; italics added].

On another occasion, and in a manner which strikingly prefigured his later metapsychological theorizing about instincts and their vicissitudes, he wrote to her:

> Since I am violent and passionate with all sorts of devils pent up that cannot emerge, they rumble about inside or else are released against you, you dear one [pp. 195–196].

This assumption of blame, through an experiential translocation of the sources of badness from his object representation of Martha into his own self-representation, repeated, we believe, the mental operations by which, as a child, he had saved and preserved the idealized image of his mother in the face of her betrayals and of his own resulting ambivalence. As we shall see in the next section, these same mental operations were to reappear later in their influence upon aspects of his theory of psychosexual development.

Jones tells us that Freud's was a successful marriage, indeed a "haven of happiness" (p. 151). In view of the travails of the engagement period this is quite remarkable, but the fact that within about a year of his marriage (1886) Freud began his relationship with Wilhelm Fliess may partially explain it. Fliess became heir to the archaic idealizing needs and underlying unconscious ambivalence conflict which Freud had formerly transferred from his mother to Martha.

Three critical circumstances contributed to Freud's need to idealize Fliess during the period of their friendship (1887-1902, see Jones 1953, and Schur, 1972). Freud's serious cardiac symptoms had eventuated in Fliess becoming his trusted physician upon whom he depended as a kind of magician-healer. Second, Freud was beginning his lonely excursions into the dark and unexplored terrain of the unconscious and increasingly felt a strong need for Fliess to fill the role of protective mentor. A third factor was Freud's growing disillusionment with his former mentor, Joseph Breuer. For an extended period Fliess functioned as Freud's sole audience, upon whose interest, encouragement, approval, and admiration Freud became absolutely dependent for his self-confidence and motivation to work. Furthermore, in order to sustain Fliess in his position of exalted judge, Freud had to endow him with unrealistically idealized attributes, such as a superb creative intellect, and a critical judgment that was beyond reproach. A few quotations from Freud's letters to Fliess, spanning ten years, will give the flavor of this attachment:

I can write nothing if I have no public at all, but I am perfectly content to write only for you [1890; Jones 1953, p. 302].

When I talked with you and remarked what you think of me, I could even have a good opinion of myself [1890; Jones 1953, p. 301].

Your praise is nectar and ambrosia to me [1894; Jones 1953, p. 298].

I am looking forward to the congresses [meetings with Fliess] as to the slaking of hunger and thirst [1896; Schur 1972, p. 105].

After each of our congresses, I have been newly fortified for weeks... [1898; Jones 1953, p. 302].

You must not refuse the duties of [being] my first audience and supreme judge [1898; Schur 1972, p. 143].

Here I live in bad temper and darkness until you come; I get rid of all my grumbles, kindle my flickering light at your steady flame, feel well again, and after your departure I again have eyes to see and what I see is beautiful and good [1899; Schur 1972, p. 192].

It is clear that Freud developed in relation to Fliess an intense narcissistic transference configuration with mirroring and idealizing components (Kohut 1971) and colored with a good deal of oral-dependent imagery. In our view this transference situation with Fliess, like the earlier one with Martha, harked back wishfully to Freud's early ideal period with his mother in which he felt himself to be the sole object of her love and admiration. With Fliess, Freud strove to revive that early blissful union with the idealized maternal object. However, the old repressed ambivalence conflict was never far below the surface. As with Martha, Freud was constantly and excessively worried about Fliess's health (see Jones 1953). Further, he was fearfully preoccupied with the danger of a train accident whenever Fliess went on a trip, and entertained terrifying thoughts of disaster whenever he did not hear from him at regular intervals (see Schur 1972). Again, this is strongly reminiscent of Freud's crisis of separation anxiety with his mother, which reflected the rumblings of an intense unconscious ambivalence conflict.

As with Martha, Freud's reactions to disappointments by Fliess are of special interest. In this connection, Schur's (1966) provision of some additional day residues and his brilliant supplementary analysis of Freud's famous "Irma dream" (1900, pp. 106–121) are most enlightening. Briefly, the additional day residues, which occurred in 1895, were as follows: At Freud's request, one of his patients, Emma, had been examined by Fliess, and the latter had recommended nasal surgery and performed the operation himself.

Emma suffered complications from the surgery, including massive hemorrhaging. Subsequently, it became known that these complications were a direct result of Fliess's serious mishandling of the surgery—he had failed to remove a piece of iodoform gauze from the area on which he had operated. Freud's immediate reaction to the discovery of Fliess's blunder was to suffer a spell of weakness, indicative of severe emotional conflict. In his first letter to Fliess after the discovery, Freud *blamed himself* for pressing Fliess to operate in a foreign city where he could not handle the aftercare. In this and a subsequent letter, Freud completely exonerated Fliess from blame, thus protecting the latter's idealized image:

> Of course no one blames you in any way... [Schur 1966, p. 58]....you are altogether innocent! [p. 63]...for me you remain the healer, the prototype of the man into whose hands one confidently entrusts one's life and that of one's family. I wanted to tell you of my misery, perhaps ask you for some advice about Emma, but not reproach you for anything. *This would have been stupid, unjustified, in clear contradiction to my feelings...* [p. 66; italics in original].

Schur demonstrates convincingly that many of the ingredients of the Emma episode reappeared as elements of the Irma dream. The dream and Freud's associations to it indicate that the blame for the Emma affair, as well as Freud's critical and contemptuous feelings, were displaced from Fliess onto two other physicians (Rie and Breuer), while the exalted position of Fliess was reaffirmed. Further, Freud interpreted the displacements in the dream as fulfilling his wish to exonerate himself from responsibility, which by implication indicates that he had *already exonerated Fliess by blaming himself.* As Schur concludes:

> But it was not only his own exculpation that he achieved; it was the *need to exculpate Fliess from responsibility* for Emma's nearly fatal complications that was probably the strongest (immediate) motive for the constellation of his dream [p. 70; italics added. See Schur 1972, for a detailed

discussion of the further vicissitudes of Freud's unresolved unconscious ambivalence in relation to Fliess].

As with Martha, the displacements and internalizations of blame through which Freud sustained his aggrandized picture of Fliess (another mother-surrogate) repeated the mental operations through which he saved and protected his early idealized image of his mother from contamination by disappointments in her and his resulting unconscious ambivalence. We shall now proceed to show how these same mental operations left their stamp on aspects of his theory of psychosexual development.

THE DEFENSIVE-RESTITUTIVE FUNCTION OF FREUD'S THEORIES

It is the hallmark of Freud's theory of psychosexual development that a person's conflicts and neurotic difficulties are to be viewed from the perspective of a reified, internal, biological factor—namely, the vicissitudes of the child's own instinctual drives and drive energies (1905), encompassed in the metapsychological concept of the id (1923a). The role of the actual treatment of the child by his parents (in particular, the mother) in the development of his personality was in large part neglected by Freud and left to a later generation of analyst to elucidate. In Freud's theoretical view of infantile development, the sources of evil were located not in the parents (mother), but rather in the child himself, in his own sexual and aggressive impulses, which emerge according to an innate, biologically predetermined sequence in relative independence of environmental influences. We would agree with Fine (1973) that this emphasis reflected Freud's wish to exonerate his parents, especially his mother. Specifically, through the relocation of the sources of badness into the child, Freud absolved his mother from blame for her betrayals of him and safeguarded her idealized image from invasions by his unconscious ambivalence. Freud's wish to banish (destroy) the treacherous mother was replaced in his theory with the child's need to repress his own evil drive derivatives. Hence, the early, terrifying vision of

Freud's mother sealed off inside a cupboard, the product of his conflictual rage at her, was defensively transformed into its metapsychological homologue—the sealed off, unconscious id.[2] In so theorizing, Freud repeated those processes through which he preserved his idealized pictures of Martha and Fliess (mother-surrogates) by internalizing the blame for their disappointing him. His central metapsychological constructions pertaining to the id and its instinctual drives and energies and their presumptively universal vicissitudes can thus be seen as defensive reifications which served to buttress and consolidate his lifelong efforts to ward off his unconscious hatred of his mother and to maintain the ambivalence-free purity of his conscious image of their relationship.

Because of the great emphasis he placed upon it, we may assume that Freud consciously identified most strongly with the simple positive Oedipus complex as he described it in the boy (1924). In this constellation, the source of all conflict lies in the boy's own unruly instinctual desires, and all his aggression is reserved for the father. Through internalization of blame and displacement of hostility the idealized image of the mother is preserved, and the relationship between mother and son remains "altogether the most perfect, the most free from ambivalence of all human relationships" (1933 [1932], p. 133). We may assume that this characterization applies to Freud's early "perfect" union with his mother, a vision of their relationship which he later strove to protect and sustain through various defensive and restitutive operations, including those which found their way into his theory-building.

Freud himself once speculated that boys may be "able to keep intact their attachment to their mother... because boys are able to deal with their ambivalent feelings towards their mother by directing all their hostility onto their father" (1931, p. 235). In view of the material we have presented, it is not surprising that in the very next sentence he completely discredited this speculation.

We would agree with Tomkins' suggestion (1963) that crucial derivatives of Freud's unconscious hostility and other negative affects in relation to his mother can be found, not in his psychology of the boy, but rather in his description of the psychosexual development of the girl. Tomkins rests his argument on an analysis of Freud's lecture on "Femininity" in the *New Introductory Lectures* (1933 [1932]). Addressing himself to the question of the girl's transition from the pre-Oedipal phallic stage to the fully blossomed Oedipal period, Freud wrote:

> We will now turn our interest on to the single question of what it is that brings this powerful attachment of the girl to her mother to an end. This, as we know, is its usual fate: it is destined to make room for an attachment to her father.... This step in development does not involve only a simple change of object. *The turning away from the mother is accomplished by hostility; the attachment to the mother ends in hate.* A hate of that kind may become very striking and *last all through life*; it may be *carefully overcompensated* later on; as a rule one part of it is overcome while another part persists [pp. 121–122; italics added].
> The reproach against the mother which goes back furthest is that she gave the child too little milk—which is construed against her as lack of love... [p. 122].
> The next accusation against the child's mother flares up *when the next baby appears* in the nursery. If possible the connection with oral frustration is preserved: the mother could not or would not give the child any more milk because she needed the nourishment for the new arrival. In cases in which the two children are so close in age that lactation is prejudiced by the second pregnancy, this reproach acquires a real basis, and it is a remarkable fact that *a child, even with an age difference of only eleven months* [!], *is not too young to take notice of what is happening.* But what the child grudges the unwanted intruder and rival is not only the suckling but all the other signs of maternal care. *It feels that it has been dethroned, despoiled, prejudiced in its rights; it casts a jealous hatred upon the new baby and develops a grievance against the faithless mother....* [We] rarely form a correct idea of the strength of these jealous impulses, of the tenacity with which they persist and of the magnitude of their influence on later

development. Especially as this jealousy is constantly receiving fresh nourishment in the later years of childhood and the *whole shock is repeated with the birth of each new brother or sister.* Nor does it make much difference if the child happens to remain the mother's preferred favourite. A child's demands for love are immoderate, they make exclusive claims and tolerate no sharing [p. 123; italics added].

The personal references here to the birth of Julius when Freud was eleven months old and to the repeated traumatic arrivals of new siblings are clear. In these descriptions of the development of the girl, who in the text becomes a "child" and an "it," we find derivatives of Freud's own repressed narcissistic rage at his "faithless mother" who had so rudely "dethroned" and "despoiled" him, despite his being—and remaining—her "preferred favourite."

Next Freud addressed himself to the question of why the girl becomes alienated from the mother while the boy does not, and he found the answer in the circumstance that "girls hold their mother responsible for their lack of a penis and do not forgive her for their being thus put at a disadvantage" (p. 124). Furthermore:

With the discovery that her mother is castrated it becomes possible to drop her as an object, so that the motives for hostility, which have long been accumulating, gain the upper hand. This means, therefore, that as a result of the discovery of women's lack of a penis they are debased in value for girls just as they are for boys and later perhaps for men [pp. 126–127].

As Tomkins (1963) points out, one might well ask why the Oedipal boy does not normally also turn in hate away from the mother as a love object on the grounds that she has no penis. Freud does not take this logical step and acknowledge that the boy too might typically hate and reject his "debased," penis-less mother; for Freud this was the pathological exception, not the rule. Instead, in Freud's view the boy's discovery of the mother's lack of a penis typically triggers his fear of castration at the hands of the father (1931, p. 233) and the dreaded vagina eventually becomes "a place of shelter for the penis" (1923b, p. 145). We find in these contrasting accounts of psychosexual development for the boy and girl evidence of a defensive splitting of the maternal imago. In Freud's description of the boy's Oedipal development, the idealized image of his mother is preserved, harking back to the golden age before she betrayed him by disturbing their perfect union with unwanted intruders. Notwithstanding a few scattered exceptions, the split-off image of the hated, faithless, depriving and disappointing mother is reserved primarily for his account of the girl's psychosexual development, where presumably it did not threaten to expose his own repressed rage at her. Further, as noted by Tomkins, the despised attributes of the repressed, split-off image of Freud's mother reappear in his conception of the inevitable outcome of female development. In Freud's view, because the girl feels herself to be already castrated, she lacks the most powerful motive enforcing superego formation, and her insufficient superego consolidation accounts for the emotional capriciousness and undeveloped sense of justice she will supposedly display as an adult (1925, pp. 257–258). In this notion of the woman's deficient superego, we see an encapsulation of Freud's unconscious grievance against the treacherous mother who, from his vantage point, capriciously dethroned him and unjustly prejudiced his rights to her exclusive love.

In short, we believe that in Freud's theory of psychosexual development not only is the source of badness transposed into the child in order to absolve the mother of blame but the good and bad aspects of the mother are also defensively kept separate in order to ward off his intense unconscious ambivalence conflict.

Freud's (1920) postulation of an innate death instinct, through which hostility becomes an internal biological necessity rather than a reaction to betrayal and disappointment, may be viewed as the final triumph of his wish to absolve his mother. In this theory, not only is the source of human aggression located in the interior of the individual, but its original and essential direction is shifted away from external objects (mother) and toward the self. Moreover, the sanctity of the idealized maternal imago is specifically shielded from the workings of this otherwise ubiquitous aggressive-destructive instinct. In *Civilization and its Discontents* (1930 [1929]) Freud wrote tellingly:

Aggressiveness... forms the basis of every relation of affection and love among people (*with the single exception, perhaps, of the mother's relation to her male child*) [p. 113; italics added].

This remarkable statement mirrors with precision the picture of Freud's early childhood disclosed by his self-analysis, in which he discovered intense ambivalence conflicts in every significant early relationship (for example, with his father, his siblings, his nurse, and his nephew John), with "the single exception" of his tie to his mother!

One cannot help but wonder about the degree to which Freud's need to exculpate his mother and preserve her idealized image influenced his clinical formulations in his work with patients. Zetzel (1966), for example, has pointed out a striking discrepancy between Freud's published account of the famous case of the "Rat Man" (1909) and his raw clinical notes. In the published article, "The father was seen as an important real object—one who interfered with or threatened his son's instinctual impulses.... The patient's mother... was only mentioned in six brief, essentially unrevealing, statements" (Zetzel 1966, p. 220). In striking contrast, Zetzel counted "more than forty references to a highly ambivalent mother-son relationship in the original clinical notes" (p. 220).

SUMMARY AND CONCLUSIONS

We have attempted to demonstrate that Freud's wish to restore and preserve an early idealized image of his mother ran through his life like a red thread, influencing his reconstructions of his early childhood history, his choice of a field of study, his important adult relationships, and his theoretical ideas. In particular, we have attempted to show that the defensive operations which Freud employed to protect the idealized vision of his mother from invasion by a deep unconscious ambivalence conflict fatefully left their mark on his theory of psychosexual development and its central metapsychological reifications, in which the sources of evil were internalized, hostility was displaced onto the father, and the split-off bad maternal image was relegated largely to the psychology of the girl.

We believe Freud's fundamental contributions to the understanding of human beings to be monumental. He illuminated the crucial importance of early sensuous and aggressive experiences in the development of personality, and he provided profound insights into the origins and consequences of those wrenching emotional conflicts in which a person's most urgent desires and cherished wishes clash against moral prohibitions or anticipations of danger. We have seen, however, that his theoretical preoccupation with these experiential states, as well as his attempts to account for them, bore the stamp of his own subjective representational world. Moreover, the metapsychological reifications through which he sought to "explain" these phenomena—his conceptions of the instinctual drives and drive energies and their presumptively universal vicissitudes—were found in part to be products of his own defensive and restitutive struggles, rooted in his own formative life experiences. Hence, the same problematic subjective influences which limited the completeness of his self-analysis of necessity also set limits to the inclusiveness and general applicability of his theoretical constructions.

NOTES

1. Jones (1953) suggests that the circumstances of Anna's birth provided a strong stimulus to Freud's interest in the problem of the origin of children. We think that this problem must have been an especially difficult and painful one for Freud, because he felt the need for a solution to it which would exculpate his beloved mother from responsibility. The true solution to the problem of the origin of children, of course, lies in a detailed understanding of human sexuality. We can therefore discern in this early situation one of the subjective sources of Freud's later fascination with and emphasis upon sexuality in his psychoanalytic researches.

2. Freud's struggle to regain his mother's exclusive adoration is in his metapsychology also transposed into the interior of the "psychic apparatus," wherein the narcissistic ego "offers itself...as a libidinal object to the id, and aims at attaching the id's libido to itself," becoming "a submissive slave who courts his master's love" (1923a, p. 57).

REFERENCES

Erikson, E. (1954). The dream specimen of psychoanalysis. *Journal of the American Psychoanalytic Association* 2:5–56.

Fine, R. (1973). *The Development of Freud's Thought*. New York: Jason Aronson.

Freud, S. (1900). Interpretation of dreams. *Standard Edition* 45: xxiii–627. London: Hogarth Press, 1953.

———— (1905). Three essays on the theory of sexuality. *Standard Edition* 7:130–243. London: Hogarth Press, 1953.

————(1909). Notes upon a case of obsessional neurosis. *Standard Edition* 10:155–249. London: Hogarth Press, 1955.

———— (1920). Beyond the pleasure principle. *Standard Edition* 18:7–64. London: Hogarth Press, 1955.

———— (1923a). The ego and the id. *Standard Edition* 19: 1–59. London: Hogarth Press, 1961.

———— (1923b). The infantile genital organization: an interpolation into the theory of sexuality. *Standard Edition* 19:141–145. London: Hogarth Press, 1961.

———— (1924). The dissolution of the Oedipus complex. *Standard Edition* 19:173–179. London: Hogarth Press, 1961.

———— (1925 [1924]). An autobiographical study. *Standard Edition* 20: 7–70. London: Hogarth Press, 1959.

———— (1925). Some psychical consequences of the anatomical distinction between the sexes. *Standard Edition* 19: 248–258. London: Hogarth Press, 1961.

———— (1927). Postcript to the question of lay analysis. *Standard Edition* 20: 251–258. London: Hogarth Press, 1959.

———— (1930 [1929]). Civilization and its discontents. *Standard Edition* 21: 64–145. London: Hogarth Press, 1961.

—— (1931). Female sexuality. *Standard Edition* 21: 225–243. London: Hogarth Press, 1961.

—— (1933–[1932]). New introductory lectures on psychoanalysis. *Standard Edition* 22: 5–182. London: Hogarth Press, 1964.

—— (1950[1892–1899]). Extracts from the Fliess papers. *Standard Edition* 1: 177–280. London: Hogarth Press, 1966.

Jones, E. (1953). *The Life and Work of Sigmund Freud, Vol. 1.* New York: Basic Books.

—— (1955). *The Life and Work of Sigmund Freud, Vol. 2.* New York: Basic Books.

Kohut, H. (1971). *The Analysis of the Self.* New York: International Universities Press.

Schur, M. (1966). Some additional "day residues" of "The specimen dream of psychoanalysis." In *Psychoanalysis—A General Psychology*, ed. R. Loewenstein, L. Newman, M. Schur, and A. Solnit, pp. 45–85. New York: International Universities Press.

—— (1972). *Freud: Living and Dying.* New York: International Universities Press.

Tomkins, S. (1963). *Affect, Imagery, Consciousness, Vol. II: The Negative Affects.* New York: Springer, pp. 511–529.

Zetzel, E. (1966). An obsessional neurotic: Freud's Rat Man. In *The Capacity for Emotional Growth*, pp. 216–228. New York: International Universities Press, 1970.

CHAPTER 3

Carl Jung

This chapter is an analysis of the relationship between the metapsychological theory and the subjective representational world of C. G. Jung. Specifically, we attempt to demonstrate that Jung's metapsychology may be viewed as the product of reifications of his own vivid experiences of configurations of primitive self- and object-representations. And further, we attempt to show that these reifications served specific defensive and reparative functions as Jung struggled to master the subjective dangers inherent in these experiences.

THE REPRESENTATIONAL WORLD
IN JUNG'S THEORY

In this section we shall attempt to deduce from the thematic structure of Jung's metapsychology the nature of the subjective representational world which it reflects. For our elucidation of his

theory we have relied on the comprehensive summary presented in
Two Essays on Analytical Psychology (1943, 1945).[1]

The Collective Unconscious and Archetypes

One of the central constructs in Jung's metapsychology is his
notion of the objective, impersonal, transpersonal, or collective
unconscious and its contents, the archetypes.

> We have to distinguish between a personal unconscious and
> an impersonal or transpersonal unconscious. We speak of the
> latter also as the collective unconscious, because it is detached
> from anything personal and is entirely universal, and because
> its contents can be found everywhere, which is naturally not
> the case with the personal contents [p. 76].
>
> The personal layer ends at the earliest memories of infancy,
> but the collective layer comprises the pre-infantile period, that
> is, the residues of ancestral life...when psychic energy
> regresses, going even beyond the period of early infancy, and
> breaks into the legacy of ancestral life, then mythological
> images are awakened: these are the archetypes. An interior
> spiritual world whose existence we never suspected opens out
> and displays contents which seem to stand in sharpest
> contrast to all our former ideas [p. 87].
>
> The collective unconscious...is an image of the world
> which has taken aeons to form. In this image certain features,
> the archetypes or dominants, have crystallized out in the
> course of time. They are the ruling powers, the gods, images of
> the dominant laws and principles, and of typical, regularly
> occurring events in the soul's cycle of experience [p. 105].

The collective unconscious and the archetypes, regarded from
the viewpoint of the representational world implicit in Jung's
theory, embody a collection of object imagos which are
experienced as dynamically active, autonomous entities operating
independently of the individual's own volitions.

> Not only are the archetypes apparently impressions of ever-
> repeated typical experiences, but, at the same time, they

behave empirically like agents that tend towards the repetition of these same experiences. For when an archetype appears in a dream, in a fantasy, or in life, it always brings with it a certain influence or power by virtue of which it either exercises a numinous or fascinating effect, or impels to action.... Owing to their specific energy—for they behave like highly charged autonomous centres of power—they exert a fascinating and possessive influence upon the conscious mind and can thus produce extensive alterations in the subject [pp. 79–80].

In regard to a patient who experienced such an archetypal image in a vision, Jung writes:

It is no longer *he* that thinks and speaks, but *it* thinks and speaks within him...transpersonal contents are not just inert or dead matter.... Rather they are living entities which exert an attractive force upon the conscious mind [pp. 153–154].

Indeed, the experience of the object imagos as autonomous living entities may reach the point where they are felt as separate personalities residing inside the self. For instance, with regard to the anima (the archetypal female image corresponding to a man's unconscious femininity), Jung states that one "is quite right to treat the anima as an autonomous personality and to address personal questions to her" (p. 212). Jung's metapsychological formulations reify such subjective experiences of object imagos as living personalities by postulating the actual, objective existence of autonomous, highly energized entities within the individual.

The objects represented in Jung's portrayals of the collective unconscious and its archetypes are in possession of extraordinary, often magical and supernatural powers, as if they were mythological figures sprung forth from the archaic past of humanity. Experientially, these are *primitive, highly aggrandized, omnipotent objects,* and they may be either omnipotently good or omnipotently bad, "divine" or "daemonic" (p. 251). This can be seen in the clinical descriptions with which Jung illustrated his theoretical ideas:

We carried the analysis of infantile transference fantasies to
the point where it became sufficiently clear, even to the
patient, that he was making the doctor his father, mother,
uncle, guardian, and teacher, and all the rest of the parental
authorities. But, as experience has repeatedly shown, still
other fantasies appear which represent the doctor as a saviour
or god-like being—naturally in complete contradiction to
healthy conscious reasoning. [p. 74].
Finally there appear forms of fantasy that possess an
extravagant character. The doctor is then endowed with
uncanny powers: he is a magician or a wicked demon, or else
the corresponding personification of goodness, a saviour
[p. 75].
Now, if the patient is unable to distinguish the personality
of the doctor from these projections, all hope of an
understanding is finally lost and a human relationship
becomes impossible. But if the patient avoids this Charybdis,
he is wrecked on the Scylla of *introjecting* these images—in
other words, he ascribes their peculiarities not to the doctor
but to himself. This is just as disastrous. In projection, he
vacillates between an extravagant and pathological deification of the doctor, and a contempt bristling with hatred. In
introjection, he gets involved in a ridiculous self-deification,
or else a moral self-laceration.... In this way he makes himself
or his partner either god or devil [p. 80].
[The patient's dreams] revealed a very marked tendency...to
endow the person of the doctor with superhuman attributes.
He had to be gigantic, primordial, huger than father, like the
wind that sweeps over the earth—was he then to be made into
a god? Or, I said to myself, was it rather the case that the
unconscious was trying to *create* a god out of the person of the
doctor....Was the urge of the unconscious perhaps only
apparently reaching out towards the person, but in a deeper
sense toward a god? [pp. 142–143].

These descriptions of "abnormal over- or under-valuations," as
Jung elsewhere puts it (p. 106), would be familiar to contemporary

analysts as referring to the therapeutic mobilization of narcissistic transference configurations characterized by the regressive activation of primitive, omnipotent object (and self) representations, in which the fantastic attributes of the objects (and self) have little to do with their real qualities as persons (see Kernberg 1975, Kohut 1971, Lachmann and Stolorow 1976).

That the concept of the collective unconscious taken as a whole subsumes experiences of omnipotent object imagos endowed with idealized, all-good, all-healing qualities is also suggested by Jung's theoretical discussions of the potentially beneficent interplay that may occur between the unconscious and the conscious mind. Specifically, the collective unconscious is said to be "co-ordinated with the conscious mind in a compensatory relationship" (p. 137). "The paradise of the collective psyche" (p. 159), with its "treasure-house of primordial images" (p. 80), is represented as an inexhaustible source which "never rests" (p. 186) and is "constantly supplying us with contents" (p. 194) which compensate for all that is deficient and provide all that is missing in the life of the conscious mind. The collective unconscious inspires in the individual a sense of self-sufficiency in that it contains "all those elements that are necessary for the self-regulation of the psyche as a whole" (p. 187). Jung's descriptions of this potentially harmonious, complementary relationship appear to us to be metaphorical representations of idyllic experiences with an omnipotent, omniscient, all-giving, and guiding object:

> The unconscious then gives us all the encouragement and help that a bountiful nature can shower upon man. It holds possibilities which are locked away from the conscious mind, for it has at its disposal all subliminal psychic contents, all those things which have been forgotten or overlooked, as well as the wisdom and experience of uncounted centuries which are laid down in its archetypal organs.... For these reasons the unconscious could serve man as a unique guide [p. 126].

By way of an analogy, Jung alludes to the origins of the idealized object imagos in the early symbiotic union with the mother:

Therefore all those who do not want to dismiss the great
treasures that lie buried in the collective psyche will strive, in
one way or another, to maintain the newly won union with the
fundamental sources of life.... This piece of mysticism... is
just as innate in every individual as the "longing for the
mother," the nostalgia for the source from which we sprang
[p. 179].

Jung makes an especially close association between the anima
archetype and images of the magically protecting and shielding
early mother. Similarly, the animus (the archetypal image
corresponding to a woman's unconscious masculinity) is linked
with images of the idealized father. Refinding and reuniting with
these archaic idealized object imagos, which "seek to return, not in
experience only, but in deed" (p. 89), instill in the individual a
feeling of "absolute, binding, and indissoluble communion with
the world" (p. 187) and a "profound intuition of the 'eternal'
continuity of the living [from which] the idea of immortality
follows legitimately..." (p. 202).

While the collective unconscious and its archetypes may
represent longed for, idealized objects which are the source of
unimaginable goodness, they may also embody object imagos
which are highly dangerous in their omnipotent, daemoniacal
powers. Hence, the archetype may act as a highly disturbing
"interior opponent" (p. 88) which "seizes hold of the psyche with a
kind of primeval force and compels it to transgress the bounds of
humanity" (p. 80). The archetypal images "may at any time burst in
upon us with annihilating force" (p. 215), such that the individual is
"swallowed up and 'wafted' clean out of the world" (p. 154) or
"crushed by the contents of the unconscious" (p. 148). "If the
unconscious simply rides roughshod over the conscious mind, a
psychotic condition develops" (p. 172), "a catastrophe that
destroyed life" (p. 173). The individual, rendered helpless by the
awesome power of the object imagos, may "drown in... an eternal
image" (p. 156), become "submerged" (p. 215), "completely
smothered" (p. 164), "engulfed in an inner vision and be lost to his
surroundings" (p. 156). Jung compares these terrifying experiences
of omnipotent, annihilating objects with the "danger of being

devoured by the monster of the maternal abyss" (p. 180), "the dark Mother" (p. 249).

Also, in marked contrast to the earlier quotations in which the collective unconscious was portrayed as a bountiful, all-giving source of sustenance, there are passages in which it is represented as a cold, uncaring, withholding, self-absorbed, and greedily devouring object:

It is characteristic of the nature of the unconscious psyche that it is sufficient unto itself and knows no human considerations. Once a thing has fallen into the unconscious it is retained there, regardless of whether the conscious mind suffers or not. The latter can hunger and freeze, while everything in the unconscious becomes verdant and blossoms [p. 227].

The collective unconscious "sucks away the libido from consciousness and leaves the latter empty" (p. 231); furthermore, it brooks no rebellious opposition from the conscious ego and demands an attitude of total submission and surrender:

If the ego presumes to wield power over the unconscious, the unconscious reacts with a subtle attack [and] casts a spell over the ego. Against this the only defense is full confession of one's weakness in the face of the powers of the unconscious. By opposing no force to the unconscious we do not provoke it to attack [p. 246].

Especially the anima—"she-who-must-be-obeyed" (p. 199)—is represented as an overpowering, enchanting, seductive, treacherous maternal presence with mysterious and bewitching powers, capable of behaving like a possessive, "jealous mistress" (p. 211) who permits the individual no other object relationships, and who demands his "inner humiliation and surrender [to] the terrors of childhood" (p. 214). The magical, malevolent power that the anima exerts over the personality resembles a state of daemoniacal possession.

An unknown "something" has taken possession...of the psyche and asserts its hateful and harmful existence undeterred...thereby proclaiming...the sovereign power of possession [p. 237].

I recognize that there is some psychic factor active in me which eludes my conscious will in the most incredible manner. It can put extraordinary ideas in my head, induce in me unwanted and unwelcome moods and emotions, lead me to astonishing actions for which I can accept no responsibility, upset my relations with other people in a very irritating way, etc. I feel powerless against this fact and...so all I can do is marvel [p. 240].

Let us now turn to the essential psychological danger posed by the ego's continuing confrontation with the power of the archetypes.

Self-Dissolution

The omnipotent object imagos which are reified in the concept of the collective unconscious pose grave threats to the individual's self-representation. Specifically, they threaten its cohesiveness (self-boundaries), its stability (self-identity), and its affective coloring (self-esteem regulation) (see Stolorow 1975). The rock-bottom danger in the representational world of Jung's metapsychology is that of the fragmentation and disintegration of the self-representation through its "regressive dissolution in the collective psyche" (p. 160), i.e., in the omnipotent object imagos.

The greatest danger of all is the premature dissolution [of the personality] by an invasion of the collective psyche...there is always a great temptation to allow collective functioning to take the place of individual differentiation of the personality. Once the personality has been differentiated...its leveling down and eventual dissolution in the collective psyche...occasions a "loss of soul" in the individual....For the development of personality, then, strict differentiation from the collective psyche is absolutely necessary, since partial or blurred differentiation leads to an immediate melting away of the individual in the collective. There is now a danger that in the analysis of the unconscious the collective and the personal psyche may be fused together, with...highly unfortunate results [p. 161].

The symptoms which, according to Jung, signal the emergence of collective contents, are familiar to the modern analyst as indices of narcissistic regression and decompensation (see Kohut 1971), i.e., of varying degrees of fragmentation of the self-representation.

An infallible sign of collective images seems to be the appearance of the "cosmic element," i.e., the images in the dream or fantasy are connected with cosmic qualities, such as temporal and spatial infinity, enormous speed and extension of movement, "astrological" associations, telluric, lunar, and solar analogies, changes in the proportions of the body, etc....The collective element is very often announced by peculiar symptoms, as for example by dreams where the dreamer is flying through space like a comet, or thinks he is the earth, or the sun, or a star; or else is inordinately large, or dwarfishly small; or has died, has come to a strange place, is a stranger to himself, is confused, mad, etc. Similarly, feelings of disorientation, of dizziness and the like, may appear along with symptoms of [self-] inflation.... Such a loss of balance is similar in principle to a psychotic disturbance ... [pp. 170–171].

The spectre of self-boundary destruction and self-object de-differentiation threatens most obviously from the omnipotently bad object, as when the individual feels crushed, annihilated, drowned, submerged, engulfed, swallowed up, devoured, or daemoniacally possessed by an archetypal figure which "so spins us about that we ... can no longer rightly distinguish between ourselves and others" (p. 68). The danger when "differentiation is obliterated" (p. 162) is that the self-representation will "vanish permanently from view in this other" (p. 164).

Threats to the self-representation lurk, not only in the dangerous, negative manifestations of the archetypes, but in the positive, idealized ones as well. For example, Jung describes patients who suffer a profound sense of self-depletion as their self-esteem collapses in the face of the grandeur of their object imagos.

> Their self-confidence dwindles and they look on with resignation at all the extraordinary things the unconscious produces.... [They] finally give up all sense of responsibility in an overwhelming realization of the powerlessness of the ego against the fate that rules it from the unconscious [p. 148].

In these patients, confrontation with the idealized object imagos "has the effect of crushing and humiliating the personality [with a] smothering of self-confidence" (p. 157), i.e., it results in massive depression.

Thus far we have described situations in which the self-representation is threatened with disintegration or depletion as a result of the ego's passivity and helplessness in relation to the object's omnipotence, whether the object is experienced as daemoniacal or idealized. However, Jung's theoretical discussions make clear that the dissolution of self-object boundaries may also occur as a consequence of the individual's more or less active wishes for merger with the idealized object and fantasies of incorporating its greatness through identification. In such cases, the de-differentiation will manifest itself in megalomanic states of grandiose self-inflation, "a feeling of superiority that may well express itself in the form of 'godlikeness'" (p. 150).

> ...since the individual steps beyond his human proportions...[he is] a little "superhuman" and therefore, figuratively speaking, godlike. If we wish to avoid the use of this metaphor, I would suggest that we speak instead of "psychic inflation." The term seems to me appropriate in so far as the state we are discussing involves an extension of the personality beyond individual limits, in other words, a state of being puffed up. In such a state a man fills a space which normally he cannot fill. He can only fill it by appropriating to himself contents and qualities which properly ... remain outside our bounds [p. 152].

Merger and identification with the idealized object may have an aggressive quality—for instance, when the individual imagines he has conquered and de-potentiated the anima and thus appropriated her "mana" to himself. He inflates himself to the stature of a "mana-personality ... endowed with magical knowledge and power" (pp. 239–240). In his image of himself "he becomes a superman, superior to all powers, a demigod in the least" (p. 241). Jung at one point cautions that self-inflation can reach such pathological proportions that "the entire personality is disintegrated" (p. 156).

Identification with the collective psyche always brings with it a feeling of universal validity—"godlikeness"—... as a consequence of which the element of differentiation is obliterated ... [p. 162].

It is important to emphasize again that both consequences of confrontation with the idealized object—grandiose self-inflation through merger, as well as depressive self-depletion—pose the ultimate threat of self-boundary destruction.

The arrogance of the one and the despondency of the other share a common uncertainty as to their boundaries. The one is excessively expanded, the other excessively contracted. Their individual boundaries are...obliterated [p. 151].

The Disunited Man

Having established that the core danger lurking in the object world, as represented in Jung's metapsychology, is that of the dissolution of the self-representation through (active or passive) relationship with an omnipotent (good or bad) object, we are now in a position to examine the connection between this danger and another central motif in Jung's theorizing—the theme of the "disunited man" (p. 28).

According to Jung, "neurosis is self-division" (p. 30). The nature of this self-division is elucidated in the context of his comparison of the Adlerian "will to power" with the Freudian libidinal or erotic instincts. In this comparison Jung reinterprets the erotic instincts as a striving for union with idealized objects, with the accompanying danger of self-dissolution through passive surrender. The "will to power," in turn, he views as a striving for grandiose self-elevation in order to "preserve the integrity of the personality" (p. 47)—a striving which, in turn, poses the dual dangers of autistic isolation and self-boundary destruction through pathological self-inflation. These two nuclear strivings operate in everyone as antagonistic opposites, so that in Jung's conceptualization "human nature bears the burden of a terrible and unending conflict between the principle of the ego [self-preservation through grandiose isolation] and the principle of instinct [union with the idealized object]" (p. 44). What is important to stress is that in the Jungian representational world, *both* of these strivings expose the individual to the ultimate threat of the disintegration of the self-representation. He faces the spectre of self-dissolution in both the "Charybdis" of surrender to the omnipotent object and the "Scylla" of self-boundary destruction through alienated self-inflation (pp. 80-81). Were the individual to pursue either of these two core strivings with unconflictual passion, he would suffer the catastrophic fate of de-differentiation and self-loss.

We can now begin to understand, in terms of the representation-al world implied by Jung's theory, the importance which he places on the principle of *enantiodromia*—"the regulative function of opposites" (p. 82). According to this principle, every tendency of the conscious ego is balanced by the development of an opposite tendency of equal strength in the unconscious psyche. For instance, a conscious longing for union with an external object (corresponding to the so-called "extraverted attitude") would be compensated by an equally strong unconscious gravitation toward grandiose self-absorption (the "introverted attitude"). While Jung recognized that "enantiodromia" in the extreme itself posed the threat of self-fragmentation, of "being torn asunder into pairs of opposites" (p. 83). he nonetheless granted it the status of a metapsychological principle, indispensible to the regulation of the endopsychic economy:

All energy can only proceed from the tension of opposites [p. 38].
There is no energy unless there is a tension of opposites ... without which no forward movement is possible. The conscious mind ... seeks its unconscious opposite, lacking which it is doomed to stagnation, congestion, and ossification. Life is born only of the spark of opposites [pp. 63–64].
There is no balance, no system of self-regulation, without opposition. The psyche is just such a self-regulating system [p. 71].

These metapsychological assertions become intelligible once we have recognized that in the representational world of Jung's theory, an unopposed passionate pursuit of either of the two nuclear strivings would lead to catastrophic experiences of self-dissolution. "Enantiodromia," the perpetual balancing of opposite tendencies of equal strength, is required to ward off self-loss (psychic death) through surrender or self-inflation, and to preserve the integrity (psychic survival) of the self-representation.

Individuation

As the ultimate danger to be warded off in the representational world of Jung's personality theory is that of self-dissolution and self-object de-differentiation, it will come as no surprise to discover that the most important task of personality development, and the ultimate goal of analytical therapy, is that of "individuation" (p. 121)—the establishment of a cohesive, bounded self-representation sharply differentiated from the omnipotent object representations.

The significance to Jung of the theme of self-object differentiation, as well as the tenuousness of the self-representation in the representational world of Jung's theory, can be inferred from his repeated emphasis on the critical importance of making a clear distinction between the self and the omnipotent object imagos—in Jung's terminology, between the individual ego and the contents of the collective unconscious. Hence, he urges that the "solution to the Scylla and Charybdis problem" of self-dissolution is that "the patient must learn to differentiate what is ego and what is non-ego, i.e., collective psyche" (p. 83).

> It is therefore absolutely essential to make the sharpest possible demarcation between the personal and impersonal attributes of the psyche [p. 104].
> It is therefore of the utmost importance in practical treatment to keep the integrity of the personality constantly in mind.... Hence it is imperative to make a clear distinction between personal contents and those of the collective psyche....Since...individuation is an ineluctable psychological requirement, we can see from the superior force of the collective what very special attention must be paid to this delicate plant "individuality" if it is not to be completely smothered [p. 164].

To be individuated is absolutely indispensable in order to liberate the self from "all states of unconscious contamination and non-differentiation" (p. 238). The goal of treatment is to "disengage the ego from all its entanglements with collectivity and the collective unconscious" (p. 239). In his discussion of the individual's attempts to distinguish himself from the anima archtype, Jung alludes, by way of an analogy, to the developmental prototype of this struggle for self-object differentiation in the child's strivings for separation and individuation from the symbiotic tie to the mother (see Mahler, Pine and Bergman 1975), and secondarily from the father—developmental tasks which are clearly incompletely achieved in the representational world we have elucidated. Consistent with this interpretation is the sensitivity Jung shows to the symbiotic element in relationships in which one partner uses the other to supplement underdeveloped aspects of his own personality.

Essentially, Jung describes two pathways along which the individual may strive for differentiation from the omnipotent object imagos. One pathway is represented by the so-called "persona." The individual attempts to create a protective shell around himself in the form of a social pose, or public mask, which endows him with a kind of personal "magical prestige" (p. 160), through which he seeks to safeguard his differentiation from the collective psyche. However, the persona is merely a specious attempt at self-object differentiation, "a semblance, a two-dimensional reality" (p. 168), which can stiffen into an empty, alienated, artificial personality, reminiscent of the "as if" functioning of patients with undifferentiated representational worlds, who resort to primitive imitations in order to experience a spurious pseudo-identity (see Deutsch 1942). The construction of the persona in an effort at pseudo-individuation results in further painful self-division, as the public and private selves are severed and experientially segregated from one another. The greatest danger lurking along this pathway, however, is again that of self-dissolution, now through total identification with and absorption into the persona, the public self. As a consequence, major sectors of the personality are dissociated from consciousness, creating intolerable endopsychic tensions and disunity. The ego, in such a state, is described as a helpless "shuttlecock" tossed about by and crushed between the "hammer and anvil" (p. 206) of external role requirements and the clamor of unconscious demands. These descriptions once again bear testimony to the precariousness of the self-representation and the urgency of the struggle for self-object differentiation in a representational world in which self-integrity is threatened both from the outside and the inner psychic depths.

In contrast to this first pathway, a pseudo-solution, Jung posits a second route leading to true individuation, which involves "liberation from identification" (p. 235); i.e., self-object differentiation and self-articulation:

The aim of individuation is nothing less than to divest the self of the false wrappings of the persona on the one hand, and the suggestive power of the primordial images on the other [p. 183].
Individuation means becoming a single, homogenous being, and, in so far as "individuality" embraces our innermost, last, and incomparable uniqueness, it also implies becoming one's own self. We would therefore translate individuation as "coming to self-hood" or "self-realization" [p. 182].
[Individuation is] the realization, in all its aspects, of the

personality originally hidden away in the embryonic germ plasm; the production and unfolding of the original potential wholeness [p. 121].

In the representational world embedded in Jung's metapsychology, an experiential world in which a precarious self is ceaselessly threatened with dissolution through contact with omnipotent objects, self-object differentiation and the achievement of a fully articulated and cohesive self-representation are by necessity posited as the ideal goal of analytical treatment. How is this to be achieved according to Jung's theory of therapy? According to Jung's formulations, there are essentially three therapeutic activities which contribute to the consolidation of a sense of self-boundedness and self-integrity.

The first involves the time-honored psychoanalytic aim of making the unconscious conscious. In Jung's therapeutic approach this aim is focused on the making conscious of the omnipotent object imagos, by permitting them to blossom in the analytic transference (see Kohut 1971). Making these imagos conscious is already a big stride in the direction of individuation, since Jung's metapsychology explicitly equates unconsciousness with non-differentiation and consciousness with differentiation:

Differentiation is the essence, the *sine qua non* of consciousness. Everything unconscious is undifferentiated, and everything that happens unconsciously proceeds on the basis of non-differentiation—that is to say, there is no determining whether it belongs or does not belong to the self [p. 217]. If [the collective] contents remain unconscious, the individual is, in them, unconsciously commingled with other individuals—in other words, he is not differentiated, not individuated [p. 237].[2]

In these equations Jung uses the concepts of the conscious mind and the unconscious psyche as reified metaphors for states of self-object differentiation and non-differentiation, respectively. It follows that Jung would consider making the unconscious object imagos conscious as an important step in their differentiation from the self-representation.

Closely intertwined with the process of making the unconscious conscious is the second therapeutic ingredient which, in Jung's terminology, involves the "transcendent function" (p. 232)—the union and harmonious fusion of opposites formerly split apart by the division of the psyche into conscious and unconscious. As a consequence of the "transcendent function," an "undivided wholeness" (p. 235) is achieved, which Jung calls "the self" (p. 250). The self is further described as a new "centre of balance" (p. 207), "the attainment of the midpoint of the personality...a point midway between the conscious and unconscious" (p. 234)—i.e., between the conscious ego and the now conscious omnipotent object imagos. This "establishment of a balance of power between two worlds" (p. 242) creates "a new equilibrium...which...ensures for the personality a new and more solid foundation" (p. 234). The self stands "suspended between formidable influences from within and without" (p. 249), "poised between two world-pictures and their darkly discerned potencies" (p. 250). This imagery, with which Jung portrays his ideal of the fully differentiated self, suggests to us a still very precarious self-representation, whose integrity and stability is sustained, much in the manner of a magnetic bearing, through an experiential state of suspension in a position equidistant from all the object-related forces that threaten it with obliteration. Thus, the Scylla-Charybdis problem of self-dissolution is tenuously solved.

The third therapeutic activity in Jung's conceptualization of the treatment process that leads to individuation involves a repeated interpretive emphasis on making sharp demarcations between the personal and the collective contents—between the self and the omnipotent objects. As the individual assimilates archetypal material into consciousness and recognizes its intrinsically collective, transpersonal nature, he finds himself confronted not with private or unique problems, but rather with something *universally human.* He thereby experiences not only a more differentiated and stable sense of selfhood, but also a renewed and deepened solidarity with the outer world.

THE PSYCHOLOGICAL ORIGINS OF JUNG'S THEORY

In order to understand the psychological sources of Jung's theory of personality, one overriding feature of his personal development must be taken into account; namely, his secret involvement as a child in a world of religious fantasy images. In his autobiography, *Memories, Dreams, Reflections,* he refers to his secret world as "the essential factor of my boyhood" (1961, p. 22).[3] Beginning at a very early age with certain anxiety-laden reflections on the nature of Jesus Christ, and continuing with an extended series of vivid fantasies, dreams, and emotionally charged symbolic games, Jung immersed himself in a private reality which he experienced as something transcendent and apart from the affairs of everyday life.

In what follows, we shall attempt to show that Jung's experience of this "other world," both as a child and an adult, bears a direct correspondence to his final formulations of the relationship between the ego and the collective unconscious. More generally, we shall describe how the concerns and personal tensions embodied in and generated by his secret preoccupations influenced and colored his metapsychological system as a whole. This section is organized into three parts. In the first, we trace the development of Jung's fantasies with a view toward disclosing the nature of his subjective representational world. In the second, we discuss the difficult and traumatically disappointing formative experiences which made his involvement in a secret world necessary. And in the third, we interpret the concepts of his metapsychology as expressions of the issues and concerns which dominated his personal existence.

The Genesis of the Secret

Jung's account of the development of his secret childhood preoccupations begins with some early reflections on the nature of Jesus Christ. At the age of three, he had been taught to say the following prayer each night before going to sleep.

> Spread out thy wings, Lord Jesus mild,
> And take to thee thy chick, thy child.
> If Satan would devour it,
> No harm shall overpower it,
> So let the angels sing [p. 10].

The prayer pictures Jesus as a protecting and child-loving figure, and Jung at first envisioned him as a nice, benevolent gentleman sitting on a throne in the sky. But the phrase, "take to thee thy chick, thy child" ("nimm dein Küchlein ein"), was confusing; one "takes" medicine, that is, swallows it. He thought the prayer meant that Jesus swallows children in order to keep the devil from eating them. The rather ominous connotations of the word "take" in this connection were reinforced by Jung's observations of funerals and burials. He witnessed several scenes in which men dressed in frock coats, top hats, and shiny black boots gathered about a hole in the ground and lowered a mysterious black box into it.

> My father would be there in his clerical gown, speaking in a resounding voice. Women wept. I was told that someone was being buried in this hole in the ground. Certain persons who had been around previously would suddenly no longer be there. Then I would hear that they had been buried, and that Lord Jesus had taken them to himself [p. 9].

Being "taken" by Jesus was somehow equivalent to being lowered into the ground. The positive and benevolent aspects of the image of Jesus began to be undermined and transformed by the sinister qualities of the men who occupied themselves with the black box.

These disturbing impressions concerning Jesus, death, and being "taken" were among the determinants of an experience which Jung describes as his "first conscious trauma" (p. 10): One day as he was playing in the sand in front of his house, he looked up and saw a figure in a broad hat and strange black garment coming down the hill toward him. It seemed to be a man who had disguised himself as a woman.

> At the sight of him I was overcome with fear, which rapidly

grew into deadly terror as the frightful recognition shot
through my mind: "That is a Jesuit." Shortly before, I had
overheard a conversation between my father and a visiting
colleague concerning the nefarious activities of the Jesuits.
From the half-irritated, half-fearful tone of my father's
remarks, I gathered that "Jesuits" meant something specially
dangerous, even for my father. Actually I had no idea what
Jesuits were, but I was familiar with the word "Jesus" from my
little prayer [p. 11].

Imagining that the approaching figure had some terrible and evil
purpose in mind, probably to kill and then devour him, Jung
rushed into his house, ran up the stairs, and hid in the darkest
corner of his attic. For days and even weeks afterward he remained
"hellishly frightened" that the Jesuit (actually a harmless Catholic
priest) might return. It was years before he could set foot inside a
Catholic church and be in the presence of priests without
experiencing an oppressive uneasiness.

The concerns embodied in Jung's childish reflections on the
nature of Jesus and in the traumatic experience with the Jesuit also
expressed themselves in a terrifying nightmare, occurring between
the ages of three and four, which became the first great secret of his
childhood. He dreamed that he was walking in a meadow and came
upon a rectangular hole in the ground. He climbed down beneath
the surface and discovered a doorway covered by a green curtain.
Curious to discover what might lie concealed behind, he pushed the
curtain aside and gazed into a long rectangular chamber which was
lined with stone. In the center of the chamber floor there was a red
carpet running from the entrance to a low platform.

On this platform stood a wonderfully rich golden
throne.... Something was standing on it which I thought at
first was a tree trunk twelve to fifteen feet high and about one
and a half to two feet thick. It was a huge thing, reaching
almost to the ceiling. But it was of a curious composition: it
was made of skin and naked flesh, and on top there was
something like a rounded head with no face and no hair. On

the very top of the head was a single eye, gazing motionlessly upward.... The thing did not move, yet I had the feeling it might at any moment crawl off the throne and creep toward me. I was paralyzed with terror. At that moment I heard from outside and above my mother's voice...."Yes, just look at him. That is the man-eater." That intensified my terror still more, and I awoke sweating and scared to death [p. 12].

Jung was haunted by this dream through the whole of his lifetime and regarded it as a revelation of a subterranean God "not to be named" (p. 13). The terrifying image of the enthroned tree reappeared in his thoughts whenever anyone around him spoke too emphatically about Jesus. A sinister and frightening dimension of being had been disclosed to his childish imagination, a dark realm of the world which was never spoken of by his parents or the other people in his environment. He had been taught to think of Jesus as a wonderfully kind figure, seated on high, a person toward whom one could be entirely trusting and positive. But from this same Jesus had come the devouring Jesuit; and in correspondence to the heavenly God of mercy and goodness, there was the revealed flesh tree which fed on the bodies of men beneath the surface of the earth. Jung had arrived at the essential images which were to form the nucleus of his early childhood secret and also the unconscious beginnings of his later intellectual life.

The fantasy image of the two-sided nature of God implicit in the above, i.e., the partial dissociation between Jesus Christ on the one hand and the Jesuit and the man-eating flesh tree on the other, appears to reflect a splitting process in which an omnipotent object imago began to divide into positive and negative components. The benevolent, sustaining, and protecting attributes of Lord Jesus were seen in stark contrast to the terrifying and devouring qualities of his negative counterparts on and under the earth. The world had been revealed in his mind as a polarized tension between above and below, omnipotent good and omnipotent evil. We can therefore discern in these images an early source of Jung's later obsession with the reconciliation of opposites, the problem of wholeness, and integration. Indeed, his late work, *Answer to Job* (1952), which is an attempt to come to terms with the dark and light aspects of the

Judeo-Christian God, is a project strikingly prefigured in the ruminations of his early childhood.

The content of the incorporative imagery we have described suggests that the core issue around which Jung's early emotional life revolved was the danger of self-obliteration through absorption (symbolized in fantasies of being devoured) by omnipotent objects. An extreme vulnerability and instability of his self-representation is further indicated in his account of his reactions to entering school, especially his susceptibility to the influence of his peers. At first, he was very happy to have playmates; the earlier period of his childhood had been spent almost entirely alone (his one sibling, a sister, was not born until he was nine). In addition, the loneliness of his life then had been immeasurably increased by the "secret" which he felt could be shared with no one. But once in school, he found himself changing in disturbing ways, and he sensed an internal division beginning to take place:

> I found that [my schoolmates] alienated me from myself. When I was with them I became different than the way I was at home...my schoolfellows...misled me or compelled me to be different from what I thought I was....It was as if I sensed an internal division beginning to take place, and feared it. My security was threatened [p. 19].

Coinciding with the frightening self-transformation and internal division generated by Jung's entering school and joining the wider social world outside of his family, he developed a set of symbolic games which shed a fascinating light on the subjective concerns dominating this period of his life (from seven to ten years). One of these involved fire. In his family's garden there was an old wall built of blocks of stone. There were spaces between the blocks which made interesting caves.

> I used to tend a little fire in one of these caves...a fire that had to burn forever....No one but myself was allowed to tend this fire. Others could light fires in other caves, but their fires were profane and did not concern me. My fire alone was living and had an unmistakable aura of sanctity about it [p. 20].

The image of the eternal living fire, the inviolable imperative that only he could tend it, and the notion that it was sacred by comparison with the profane fires of other boys appear to us to symbolize a beginning partial solution to the crisis of identity he was then experiencing. The danger of self-loss through immersion in the powerful influences of the wider social environment was warded off through the compensatory elaboration of a private, aggrandized, and immortalized self-identity transcending the "profane" world of his peers.

A second game involved a curious relationship with a stone. Often, when he found himself alone, Jung sat down on a special stone which jutted out from the same slope on which he tended his sacred fire. A dialogue would then begin, reflecting his difficulties and struggles with self-object differentiation.

> "I am sitting on the stone and it is underneath." But the stone could also say, "I am lying here on this slope and he is sitting on top of me." The question then arose: "Am I the one sitting on the stone or am I the stone on which *he* is sitting?"... The answer remained totally unclear, but there was no doubt whatsoever that this stone stood in some secret relationship to me [p. 20].

Jung was especially likely to go to his stone when he felt confused and in conflict because of his perpetual brooding on the secret revelations of his earlier childhood (the Jesuit, the man-eater, etc.). He frequently felt a powerful longing to communicate these experiences to someone and break out of the psychological isolation into which his secret knowledge had plunged him. At the same time, however, he feared a disclosure of his inner thoughts would meet with incomprehension, shock, and ridicule. At such times, the stone made him feel strangely calmed and reassured.

> "The stone has no uncertainties, no urge to communicate and is eternally the same for thousands of years," I would think.... I was but the sum of my emotions, and the Other in me was the timeless, imperishable stone [p. 42].

The stone can therefore be seen as a symbolic equivalent of the eternal sacred fire. Both objects served the narcissistic reparative function of solidifying and stabilizing a precarious self-representation by supporting the formation of an entirely independent, immortalized, and grandiose self-image. The fact that such games developed at all underlines the profound difficulty he was then experiencing in maintaining a stable sense of self-integrity. Jung's self-representation remained vulnerable to pressures and influences from the external social milieu throughout his life. This is illustrated especially clearly in his later travels to Africa, where he felt threatened by the intensity of life in an alien environment and repeatedly envisioned the dreadful fate of losing his European identity and "going black under the skin" (p. 245).

All of the issues and concerns which we have been discussing were brought together in a last game which Jung describes as "the climax and conclusion of my childhood" (p. 22). A drastically increasing sense of inner disunion and a growing uncertainty about his position in the world at large led him one day during his tenth year to carve and paint a little wooden manikin. It was two inches long, with a frock coat, top hat, and shiny black boots. He put the manikin in a pencil case, where he had prepared a little bed for it.

> In the case I also placed a smooth oblong blackish stone from the Rhine, which I had painted with water colors to look as if it were divided into an upper and lower half....This was *his* stone. All this was a great secret. Secretly I took the case to the forbidden attic at the top of the house...and hid it with great satisfaction on one of the beams under the roof—for no one must ever see it!...No one could discover my secret and destroy it. I felt safe, and the tormenting sense of being at odds with myself was gone. In all difficult situations...I thought of my carefully bedded down and wrapped up manikin and his smooth, prettily colored stone [p. 21].

Jung's little manikin, hidden away in the attic with a stone all its own, became the cardinal secret of his childhood existence. He imagined that his life depended on preventing anyone from ever discovering it. Similarly, he never told anyone about the Jesuit or the underground man-eater, for they too were a part of that mysterious realm from which the gaze of the world was barred. At the same time, the fashioning of the manikin represented an attempt to give his secret a tangible form and to discover for himself exactly what it was. It is one of the fascinating paradoxes of Jung's childhood that he was driven to secrecy and concealment while at the same time never knowing the precise content of that which he was protecting.

We believe that Jung's own hidden self was his deepest secret and that his elaborate precautions to conceal and hide his thoughts and symbolic actions constituted defensive attempts to ward off self-loss through merger with objects. This interpretation is interestingly confirmed by a passage which occurs near the end of his autobiography.

> There is no better means of intensifying the treasured feeling of individuality than the possession of a secret which the individual is pledged to guard [p. 342].

The ritual of the manikin appears to us to have had a dual significance for Jung. In the first place, it was painted black and decorated to resemble the Jesuit and the ominous looking men whom he had earlier watched lowering black boxes into the ground (the lair of the man-eater). His actions therefore amounted to a concretization and symbolic encapsulation of the object-related forces to which his self-representation was still so vulnerable. Since the manikin was Jung's personal secret, charged in his mind with the overwhelming power he had earlier experienced as residing in the object world outside of himself, the ritual reflects a striving to gain mastery over the omnipotence of objects and ensure the stability and integrity of his self-representation. We can characterize the manikin in this respect as a *transitional self-object,* analogous in function to the class of imaginary friends discussed by Bach (1971). Indeed, it became a powerful source of security in Jung's early life and assisted him in maintaining his stability in the face of what otherwise might have been unendurable situations. Whenever he had done something wrong or his feelings had been hurt, or when he felt oppressed by his father and mother, his thoughts would turn to the treasured secret in the attic.

In the second place, Jung *identified* with the manikin and its immortal stone, and thereby appropriated a share of their aggrandized powers for himself. In this context the ritual emerges as a symbol of a profound withdrawal from external object ties into a sealed-off world of self-sufficiency and omnipotent splendor. The isolation which his defenses imposed upon him, however, created what he describes as "an almost unendurable loneliness" (p. 41), and as a consequence he was constantly longing for an opportunity to share his strange experiences with other human beings. The reassurance provided by his secret existence of grandeur and immortality came at the price of terrible feelings of alienation and estrangement from his family, his peers, indeed, from the whole of humanity. Thus, we can see in this nuclear situation the crystallization of a conflict which came to pervade his whole life; namely, the conflict between an impelling need to sever object ties and retreat into a grandiose world of secrecy in order to prevent self-loss through merger with objects; and the longing to repair object ties and reestablish communication with others in order to ward off self-extinction through unendurable isolation and loneliness.

The solution to Jung's conflict which appeared during his adolescence involved a paradoxical situation in which he found it possible to be involved in relationships with other persons while at the same time remaining safely protected from dangers to the self through participation in a secret realm of grandiose fantasies. A dual mode of existence came into being in which his self-image split apart into two separately personified components. "Personality No. 1," as he called one of these components, was the outer self which was known to his parents and other persons; this was the self for which social ties and external reality were of the greatest significance. "Personality No. 2," on the other hand, was a hidden self which was unknown to others and which entertained secret fantasies about the ultimate mysteries of the cosmos. Jung experienced his No. 2 personality as belonging to a world other than the one in which he lived as a child; he variously imagined it as an immensely old man, a dignified and important gentleman from the eighteenth century, a potentate in a fortress protected by cannons, and sometimes even as an ageless being who existed outside of time and enjoyed the majestic status of God. By periodically entering No. 2's secret and secure world of cosmic feelings and images, he was able to escape the painful interpersonal situations in which his No. 1 personality became involved. In addition to the life he shared with other human beings,

> there existed another realm, like a temple in which everyone who entered was transformed and suddenly overpowered by a vision of the whole cosmos, so that he could only marvel and admire, forgetful of himself.... Here nothing separated man from God; indeed, it was as though the human mind looked down upon creation simultaneously with God [p. 45].

Jung's choice of a career in psychiatry represented a compromise between the conflicting streams of interest which were personified in his twofold self-image. The influence of "personality No. 2" drove him to pursue philosophy, religion, mythology, and related subjects within the humanities; "personality No. 1" became manifest in pragmatic concerns for his financial security and in interests in the more mundane subjects of science and medicine. By entering psychiatry, and particularly by specializing in the symbolic productions of the mentally ill, he was able to secure the best of both worlds. He describes the personal feelings generated by his career choice with glorious enthusiasm.

> It was as though two rivers had united and in one grand torrent were bearing me inexorably toward distant goals. This confident feeling that I was a "united double nature" carried me as if on a magical wave [p. 109].

His entire life was dominated by the play and counter-play between the two sides of his personality. During some periods No. 1 would take the ascendancy and he would become actively involved with other people and professional work. This was the case during his psychiatric training and especially during his collaboration with Freud. At such times his secret preoccupations with fantasy images seemed senseless and unreal. At other times, however, the grandiose private world of No. 2 would gain in strength and on some occasions even threaten to overwhelm his capacity to relate to external reality. Following on the traumatic break with Freud, for example, there was a resurgence of No. 2 so powerful he began to feel "menaced by a psychosis" (p. 176), "as if gigantic blocks of stone were tumbling down upon me" (p. 177).

> ...my feelings and intuitions...occurred in No. 2 personality, while my active and comprehending ego remained passive and was absorbed into the sphere of the "old man" who belonged to the centuries. I experienced him and his influence in a curiously unreflective manner; when he was present, No. 1 personality paled to the point of non-existence, and when the ego that became increasingly identical with No. 1 personality dominated the scene, the old man, if remembered at all, seemed a remote and unreal dream [p. 68].

Critical Formative Experiences

We have seen in the last section that the central issues of Jung's personal existence were those of self-preservation and self-loss—in his own terms, individuation versus the loss of individuality. Let us now review the early formative experiences which played a role in establishing and magnifying these concerns.

Not surprisingly, his earliest memories concern events which one would expect to interfere with the fundamental processes of self-object differentiation and self-articulation; namely, a traumatic disruption of the tie between himself and his mother. During his first years there were severe marital problems between his parents, and as a consequence it became necessary for his mother to leave home and spend several months in a sanitarium. This was in 1878, during the third year of his life. He experienced his mother's disappearance as an abandonment:

> I was deeply troubled by my mother's being away. From then on, I always felt mistrustful when the word "love" was spoken...The feeling I associated with "woman" was for a long time that of innate unreliability [p. 8].

Jung's tie with his mother was never fully repaired: "At bottom, she was always a stranger to me" (p. 112). Her absence from home lasted several months and seems to have produced in Jung a lasting wish for a regressive restoration of their original relationship. The literal fulfillment of this wish, i.e., the reestablishment of an early idealized symbiotic tie, however, would have entailed the relinquishment of his nascent sense of individuality as the boundaries separating self- and object-representations dissolved. This, as we have seen in all of the earlier sections of this chapter, was a danger against which Jung struggled for his entire life.

By Jung's account it appears that his mother suffered from intermittent depressions after she returned home. In addition, the tensions between her and the father persisted, sometimes growing so strong that "the atmosphere in the house was unbreathable" (p. 19). Jung's descriptions of his own attitude toward her bear a remarkable resemblance to the childish thoughts on Jesus Christ which we discussed earlier. During the daytime he experienced her as loving, companionable, and as having a hearty warmth. But at night, she acquired a set of frightening and uncanny qualities which were the source of numerous anxiety dreams.

> One night I saw coming from her door a faintly luminous indistinct figure whose head detached itself from the neck and floated along in front of it, like a little moon. Immediately another head was produced and detached itself [p. 18].
> By day she was a loving mother, but at night she seemed uncanny. Then she was like one of those seers who is at the same time a strange animal, like a priestess in a bear's cave. Archaic and ruthless; ruthless as truth and nature [p. 50].

Hence, in Jung's early experience of his mother, we see glimpses of the developmental origins of the split omnipotent object imagos which dominated his representational world—and his metapsychology.

Later in his childhood he came to imagine that the uncanny qualities of his mother expressed something analogous to his own secret, and he entertained the notion that she too possessed a No. 1 and No. 2 personality. This idea was never something he could talk

openly about with her, but it nevertheless gave him reassurance
and a small measure of relief from his terrible loneliness.

His relationship with his father was different. The father was a
parson; according to Jung's descriptions, he suffered from painful
religious doubts and consequently adhered dogmatically to the
teachings of his church. It was therefore pointless to tell his father
of the burning revelations which were constantly haunting him.
Only once did Jung allow himself to think he could discuss
something related to his secret thoughts. His father had been
instructing him on the catechism as a preparation for confirma-
tion. Jung came across a passage dealing with the mystery of the
Holy Trinity, and it immediately engaged his attention.

> Here was something that challenged my interest: a oneness
> that was simultaneously a threeness. This was a problem that
> fascinated me because of its inner contradiction. I waited
> longingly for the moment when we would reach this question.
> But when we got that far, my father said, "We now come to the
> Trinity, but we'll skip that for I understand nothing of it
> myself."...I was profoundly disappointed and said to myself,
> "There we have it; they know nothing about it and don't give it
> a thought. Then how could I talk about my secret?" [p. 53].

Clearly, the relationship with his father failed to provide a
substitute for the lost idealized tie to the mother. The alienation
between himself and his father was not the only factor serving to
intensify his terrible sense of isolation and estrangement from
other people. He wanted more than anything else someone to talk
with, someone with whom he could find a sense of understanding
and communion.

> ...nowhere did I find a point of contact; on the contrary, I
> sensed in others an estrangement, a distrust, an apprehension
> which robbed me of speech. That, too, depressed me. I did not
> know what to make of it. Why has no one had experiences
> similar to mine? I wondered....Am I the only one who has had
> such experiences? Why should I be the only one? It never
> occurred to me that I might be crazy, for the light and

darkness of God seemed to me facts that could be understood even though they oppressed my feelings [p. 63].

In addition to meeting reactions of incomprehension and anxiety whenever he alluded to his secret world, Jung began to feel singled out and rejected by his peers, as if he possessed repulsive and weird traits. He was driven to seek companionship among the dullest of the students.

I had a liking for those who were none too bright.... They had something to offer which I craved deeply: in their simplicity they noticed nothing unusual about me [p. 64].

The painful idea that he was being shunned on account of his own disagreeable and repellent qualities was drastically reinforced one day when he was falsely accused of cheating and utterly humiliated before all the other children in his class (p. 64).

A last childhood experience which must have served to further undermine Jung's trust in others is briefly mentioned in a letter to Freud. In an attempt to analyze the anxiety and reserve characterizing his attitude toward Freud as a person, he describes how he was once sexually molested by an older man whom he had idolized and worshipped (McGuire 1974, p. 95). Such an incident, even though not dealt with in his autobiography, must have been a further shattering, searing trauma, and one can easily imagine how powerfully it would have strengthened his need to retreat from others and establish an entirely self-sufficient mode of existence.

The Subjectivity of Jung's Theories

The first part of this chapter was devoted to translating Jung's concepts into phenomenological terms and to understanding the nature of the representational world implicit in Jungian theory. This is a world, it was seen, in which the individual is engaged in a perpetual struggle to defend the integrity and stability of his self-representation against the danger of annihilation through merger with omnipotent object imagos. The review of Jung's childhood development disclosed (not surprisingly) that this struggle was also the central issue of his personal existence.

The metapsychological image of the ego as situated between (and endangered by) two vast collectives—one in the depths of the unconscious and the other in society—mirrors the profound bifurcation of Jung's personal subjective world into its No. 1 and No. 2 realms. In addition, his conception of the psychodynamic process as an interplay between the reciprocally antagonistic motives of the "will to power" and Eros directly corresponds to Jung's own deepest conflict; namely, the conflict between the need to preserve himself through withdrawal into grandiose isolation and self-elevation (power) and the need to repair severed object ties and recover a disrupted sense of union with objects (Eros). His descriptions of the two directions of flow of the libido—introversion and extraversion—also constitute derivatives of this central conflict (see the discussion of Jungian-type theory in Atwood and Tomkins 1976).

The division and polarized tension inherent in Jung's personality also manifested itself in his theory of dreams, and particularly in the principles by which he believed dreams should be interpreted. The dream, like the ego, is understood as a psychological entity standing between and simultaneously embedded in two worlds: the individual's external interpersonal situation on the one hand, and the internal structure and dynamics of his psyche on the other. Accordingly, a full and adequate study of dreams must proceed in two directions: objective and subjective.

> Interpretation on the objective level is analytic, because it breaks down the dream content into complexes of memory that refer to external situations. Interpretation on the subjective level is synthetic, because it detaches the underlying complexes of memory from their external causes, regards them as tendencies or components of the subject, and reunites them with that subject [1943, 1945, p. 94].

Jung's system of metapsychology, however, was something more than just a mirror of his subjective experiences; it also served several specific defensive and reparative functions made necessary by the problematic issues crystallized during his childhood. In the reified concept of the collective unconscious, for example, his theory asserts that the aggrandized obliterating power with which external objects may be endowed derives not from the objects themselves, but rather from the deep layers of the individual's own mind. The dangerousness of relating to external objects is therefore eliminated by a transposition of their omnipotence into the unconscious psyche. In a telling passage Jung comments:

> The recognition of the archetypes takes us a long step forwards. The magical or daemonic effect emanating from our neighbor disappears when the mysterious feeling is traced back to a definite entity in the collective unconscious [1943, 1945, p. 107].

The collective unconscious can therefore be viewed as a device serving to rob the daemoniacal, magically threatening objects of their frightening qualities. The obliterating power residing in the external world is experientially relocated into the interior of the psyche, endowing its possessor with a sense of borrowed omnipotence. Indeed, Jung's conceptualization of the collective unconscious *per se* portrays a "self-contained world" (1943, 1945, p. 194) in which all sources of goodness and badness reside inside the personality, and the individual is thereby protected from both dependence on and vulnerability to powerful external objects. We can understand that such self-insulating defenses were necessary to ward off the ultimate danger of self-dissolution inherent in Jung's representational world, wherein a fragile self-representation was perpetually threatened by omnipotent object imagos with annihilation. The reification of the concept of the collective unconscious bears a striking analogy to the function of the manikin of Jung's childhood. The fashioning and hiding away of the manikin in its little pencil case, it will be recalled, was a concretization and psychological encapsulation of the destructive powers which Jung was then experiencing as emanating from the external object world. By concretizing, localizing, and thus isolating these powers, Jung protected his vulnerable self-representation from the catastrophic fate of dissolution in the influences of his social environment.

In addition to depotentiating the object world, the manikin also functioned as a transitional self-object, conferring on Jung's experience of himself a badly needed sense of integrity and temporal continuity. In the same way, his work on the theory of the collective unconscious represented an attempt to prove that the finite and fragile phenomenon of individual consciousness rests upon and derives from a timeless, imperishable foundation located deep within the psyche. By reifying the image of this interior foundation and by trying to demonstrate its reality through empirical investigation, Jung transformed a fantasized source of stability, continuity, and transcendence into an actual, objective entity existing independently of the troubled world of external-object relationships. Contact with the collective unconscious (as with the stone of Jung's childhood) provided a sense of eternity, changelessness, and stability transcending the threatening forces of the interpersonal milieu.

But the theory of the collective unconscious is more than just an intellectual parallel of the manikin and the immortal stone; it is also an affirmation that this timeless foundation deep within the psyche is transpersonal and universal. In the section on Jung's childhood we discussed how his defensive withdrawal into grandiose isolation came at the price of almost unendurable feelings of loneliness and estrangement from others. He repeatedly questioned why no one else had experiences such as his, and why his tentative attempts to break out of the isolation of his secret world always met with such dismal failure. His bold assertion that the collective unconscious is universal and transpersonal represents in this context an intellectual realization of his desire to emerge from his encapsulated singularity and repair his ruptured ties to the external object world by establishing a bond with the rest of humanity.

It was clear to me from the start that I could only find contact with the outer world and with people if I succeeded in

showing—and this would demand the most intensive effort—
that the contents of psychic experience are real, and real not
only as my own personal experiences, but as collective
experiences which others also have. Later, I tried to
demonstrate this in my scientific work, and I did all in my
power to convey to my intimates a new way of seeing things. I
knew that if I did not succeed, I would be condemned to
absolute isolation [pp. 194–195].

We are now in a position to understand the subjective sources of
Jung's emphasis on integration and on the union of opposites as
the ultimate fulfillment of the human potential. From the fact that
his subjective world was organized around the wrenching issues of
self-dissolution, self-division, and never-ending conflict, it follows
that his ideal self-image would be one of integrated harmony,
reconciliation, and transcendent wholeness. In his theory of the
process of individuation, this personal image of self-cohesion was
transformed and universalized into a metapsychological conception of the goal of human development in general.

SUMMARY AND CONCLUSIONS

We have demonstrated that Jung's metapsychology may be
fruitfully analyzed as a psychological product mirroring his
subjective representational world, and that the central reifications
of his theoretical system served his most urgent defensive and
reparative requirements. We believe that his contributions to
understanding human experience were important ones. Their
principal significance, however, emerges most clearly when they
are stripped of metapsychological reifications and retranslated
into phenomenological terms. His life work then becomes a
fascinating descriptive psychology of the vicissitudes and transformations of primitive self- and object-representations and their
typical symbolizations in the analytic transference, in the
spontaneous productions of individuals, and in the store of
mythological and religious imagery which is the heritage of
mankind as a whole.

NOTES

1. Unless otherwise indicated, all references in this section are from this work.

2. We might note that these equations are questionable; one may be unconscious of differentiated representations and conscious of undifferentiated representations.

3. All references in this section, unless otherwise indicated, are from this autobiography.

REFERENCES

Atwood, G., and Tomkins, S. (1976). On the subjectivity of personality theory. *Journal of the History of the Behavioral Sciences* 12:166–177.

Bach, S. (1971). Notes on some imaginary companions. *Psycho-analytic Study of the Child* 26:159–171.

Deutsch, H. (1942). Some forms of emotional disturbances and their relationship to schizophrenia. *Psychoanalytic Quarterly* 11:301–321.

Jung, C.G. (1943, 1945). *Two Essays on Analytical Psychology.* Cleveland and New York.: Meridian Books, 1965.

———(1952). Answer to Job. In *Collected Works of C.G. Jung, Vol. 11: Psychology and Religion: West and East.* New York.: Bollingen Foundation, 1963.

———(1961). *Memories, Dreams, Reflections.* New York.: Vintage Books, 1965.

Kernberg, O. (1975). *Borderline Conditions and Pathological Narcissism.* New York.: Jason Aronson.

Kohut, H. (1971). *The Analysis of the Self.* New York.: International Universities Press.

Lachmann, F., and Stolorow, R. (1976). Idealization and grandiosity: developmental considerations and treatment implications. *Psychoanalytic Quarterly* 45:565–587.

Mahler, M., Pine, F., and Bergman, A. (1975). *The Psychological*

Birth of the Human Infant. New York.: Basic Books.
McGuire, W., ed. (1974). *The Freud/Jung Letters.* Princeton, N.J.: Princeton University Press.
Stolorow, R. (1975). Toward a functional definition of narcissism. *International Journal of Psycho-Analysis* 56:179–185.

CHAPTER 4

Wilhelm Reich

This chapter is a psychobiographical analysis of the life and work of Wilhelm Reich. A number of studies of Reich have been published in recent years (Rycroft 1969, Reich 1970, Wycoff 1973, Boadella 1974), and while some of them contain suggestions as to the role of certain personal experiences in his thought, none attempts to thoroughly investigate the relationship between the evolution of his theories and the organization of his subjective world. Our thesis is that Reich's theoretical system reflects and symbolizes a profound personal struggle which is traceable to his childhood experience of his mother's suicide. The impact of this primal tragedy will be seen in the structure of his ideas on an extraordinary number of subjects, ranging from the causes and treatment of psychological disturbances to the phenomenon of unidentified flying objects.

There are three interdependent thematic elements which run through all of Reich's work and structure his metapsychological conceptions: (1) the notion that the expression of sexuality coincides with the expression and functioning of life in general; (2)

the notion that the life-sexual functions are being perpetually suppressed and distorted by anti-sexual death forces in the world; and (3) the notion that he, by an inner messianic imperative, be the champion of life and sexuality in their struggle against the forces of death. The first part of this chapter documents the pervasiveness of this thematic structure by briefly reviewing those aspects of his work in which it is most clearly manifest. The second part describes his childhood and defines the probable relationship between his theories and the circumstances surrounding his mother's death. The third part deals with certain other aspects of his work which shed a fuller light on the organization of his subjective representational world and the overall course of his life.

THEMATIC STRUCTURE OF REICH'S WORKS

Character Analysis and Orgastic Potency

Reich's professional career began during the early 1920s when he became interested in sexology and Freudian psychoanalysis. Even earlier he was convinced of the supreme significance of sexuality in human affairs. An entry in his diary of 1919 reads: "Sexuality is the center around which revolves the whole of social life as well as the inner life of the individual" (1942a, p. 4).

After a few years of psychoanalytic experience, Reich formulated his overriding conception of human neurotic illness, a conception according to which the energy of neurotic symptoms is always a derivative of a *stasis* of sexuality. He believed the cardinal symptom of all neurotic persons consisted in an incapacity to experience sexual impulses and sexual activity in a natural and uninhibited way. The theory of sexual stasis led to the correlated concept of "orgastic potency" as the ultimate criterion of psychological well-being. Reich defined orgastic potency as follows:

... the capacity for surrender to the flow of biological energy without any inhibiton... for complete discharge of all dammed up sexual excitation through pleasurable contractions of the body [1942a, p. 79].

It was also during this early period that he came to the theory of character armor and to the psychotherapeutic method known as character analysis. Reduced to its simplest terms, character armor consists in a stratified system of defenses which is initially set up to protect the ego against internal and external dangers. This defensive system is acquired from pathogenic childhood experiences and manifests itself not only in isolated neurotic symptoms, but in a patient's "whole character," i.e., in his characteristic general mode of reacting and behaving, including muscular expressions and posture. Character analysis as an active therapeutic technique focuses on the patient's typical ways of resisting and defending himself against unconscious material, and against analytic insight. It aims at dissolving the armor, layer by layer, and freeing the patient's deeply suppressed bio-sexual impulses. In this connection Reich speaks of the "crystallizing out of the genital object libido" as the goal of his psychotherapeutic procedures. The establishment of orgastic potency was the criterion for the success of a character analysis.

Many of the concepts and technical recommendations presented in Reich's book *Character Analysis* (1933a) have been of great value in the development of psychoanalysis. At the same time the contents of this work bear the unmistakable stamp of his personality. If we visualize him operating as a therapist within this scheme of ideas, a triangular situation emerges which mirrors the thematic structure described in the introduction to this paper. There is first of all the patient's deeply suppressed capacity for full emotional and sexual expression (later characterized as the patient's "biological core"); second, there is the defensive but ultimately pathological armor which is set up against these capacities (the suppressing death force); and third, there is Reich himself as therapist dissolving the armor and freeing the patient to discharge sexuality and live in a spontaneous and natural way.

Political Thought

During the second half of the 1920s, Reich's interests turned from an exclusive preoccupation with the treatment of individuals to the broader problem of social reform. He had grown disillusioned with individual psychotherapy because the results he was obtaining were limited and because the number of persons who could be helped by this method was necessarily small. He began to think that the only real cure for neurosis lay in a comprehensive program of prevention. The condition of being severely armored, as he then understood it, was ubiquitous in European society. Furthermore, the armor was being perpetually recreated in the young by the equally pervasive pathogenic practices of child-rearing. He considered the widespread restrictions imposed on the sexual life of children and adolescents to be the most pernicious of these practices.

Reich theorized that there was an intimate connection between family life and the socialization of children on the one hand, and the political and economic structure of society on the other. Blending his own revisions of Freudian theory with certain ideas taken from the writings of Marx and Engels, he came to the conclusion that the process of economic repression which had been exposed by Marxist sociology was mirrored and supported by the process of sexual repression which had been the point of origin for the discoveries of psychoanalysis. Conversely, he thought the solution to the problem of sexual repression would necessarily require revolutionary change in the economic structure of society. In the essay "The Imposition of Sexual Morality" (1932), for example, he writes:

the sexual suffering among the masses is only to be resolved by means of the proletarian mass movement—to be precise, through the context of revolutionary struggle against economic exploitation...the effects of thousands of years of sexual repression [are] only to be superseded, and a gratifying sexual life to eliminate the plague of neuroses from the masses [is] only to be established, when the socialist economy has been put together and consolidated and the material prerequisites of the populace guaranteed [pp. 101–102].

Economically and politically repressive regimes, according to Reich, require submissive attitudes on the part of the governed in order to survive and flourish. He saw these attitudes as inculcated in children through the institution of the patriarchal authoritarian family. In *The Mass Psychology of Fascism*, first published in 1933, he argued:

> The interlacing of the socioeconomic structure with the sexual structure of society... takes place in the first four or five years and in the authoritarian family.... Thus the authoritarian state gains an enormous interest in the authoritarian family: It becomes the factory in which the state's structure and ideology are molded [1933b, p. 30].

The primary way in which the family prepares children for life in an authoritarian fascist state is by means of imposing a severe moral inhibition on the natural expression of sexuality. This impairment of sex makes the child afraid, shy, fearful of authority, obedient, and docile. In short, Reich regarded the social aim of sexual repression as the production of acquiescent subjects who are adjusted to the authoritarian order. Man's willingness to be economically exploited and to submit to fascist authority is created "by the embedding of sexual inhibitions and fear in the living substance of sexual impulses" (p. 30).

Reich's interest in revolutionizing society for the sake of a healthier sexuality was not restricted to theoretical statements. In 1928 he became a member of the Communist Party, participating in demonstrations, helping in the distribution of leaflets, and speaking to youth groups. At that time he seemed to have believed that a socialist revolution would overthrow the ruling classes, transform the economic and political order, and thereby remove the necessity for sexual oppression of the young. He eventually became disillusioned with the possibility of changing the world through political action. But this phase of his life continued the themes which appeared in his early clinical work. His struggle to liberate sexuality from its constraints had shifted from the individual patient to the patient's society. The anti-sexual death forces now included not only the armor, but also the social processes and institutions which he held responsible for its creation—the patriarchal family, economic repression, and fascism.

Biological Research and the Treatment of Cancer

Reich's messianic alliance with life and sexuality also manifested itself in his purely biological research. After he had been expelled from the Communist Party in 1933 (because of his emphasis on sexuality) and from the International Psychoanalytic Association in 1934 (in part because of his association with Communism), his interests turned increasingly toward cell biology. The reason for this change of fields was that he thought certain rhythmic and pulsatory phenomena characterizing the orgasm reflex were also present and could be studied in the life processes of one-celled organisms.

A series of "observations" convinced him that he had identified two microscopic particles which were intimately involved in the creation and destruction of life at the cellular level. These were the so-called PA (packet-amoeboid) bions and the T (Tod, meaning death)-bacilli. Briefly, the former were spherical blue bodies which appeared following the disintegration of healthy tissue and, under certain conditions, from inorganic materials such as sand. PA bions were "shown" to cluster together and sometimes even to spontaneously organize themselves into forms displaying all the basic properties of life. The T-bacilli, on the other hand, were smaller lancet-shaped particles generated from the disintegration of diseased and putrefied tissues. They attacked healthy cells, but seemed to be neutralized when the blue bions were present. Injections of solutions containing large numbers of T-bacilli were reported to give rise to cancerous tumors in mice. When PA bions were mixed in solution with T-bacilli, however, the injections produced no harmful effects. Reich concluded that the deadly carcinogenic power of the T-bacilli was being counteracted by the presence of the blue bions. Furthermore, when bions generated from sand were placed in the presence of cancer cells,

they killed or paralyzed the cells even at a distance of approximately 10 microns...the amoeboid cancer cells would remain rooted on one spot as though paralyzed; then they would spin around frantically and, finally, become motionless [1948, p. 82].

These and a series of related "observations" formed a point of departure for Reich's work on the origin and treatment of cancer in human patients. In embarking on studies of cancer he at first thought he was breaking away from his earlier concern with the problem of sexuality. Experience with patients suffering from this disease, however, quickly convinced him of the contrary. His cancer patients seemed invariably to be suffering from pathology in the sexual sphere, and he therefore argued that "the confusing variety of manifestations presented by the cancer disease only hides a common basic disturbance...sexual stasis" (1942b, p. 230). He theorized that the blocking of sexuality involved a "biopathic shrinking" process in which life energy was withdrawn from various parts of the body and immobilized. These devitalized parts then tended to putrefy, generate the deadly T-bacilli, and eventually become predisposed to develop cancer.

The bion studies which led to Reich's interest in cancer also played an important role in the development of his conception of the "orgone" energy. Optical and electrical phenomena of various kinds were "observed" in the immediate neighborhood of the PA bion cultures. This suggested that bio-energetic radiations were emanating from the cultures, and Reich thought these radiations were directly involved in the anti-cancer effects he had observed earlier. When he found that the optical and electrical phenomena occurred independently of the presence of the PA bion cultures, he boldly concluded that the life-supporting radiations were present everywhere in the earth's atmosphere. This was the origin of the all-pervading orgone energy.

Reich never claimed to have found a cure for cancer, but he did report that orgone irradiation had positive effects on the course of the disease. In *The Cancer Biopathy* (1948) he describes a number of patients whose conditions were improved in varying degrees through treatments in the "orgone energy accumulator," a chamber specially designed to concentrate the free orgone in the atmosphere.

Reich's concerns with the suppression of life and sexuality can be
seen to have undergone a massive generalization during the phase
of his biological studies. The effects of sexual stasis now included
the creation of deadly physical diseases. Thus a direct line of
causality ran from fascism in the political structure of society, to
carcinogenic T-bacilli in the microscopic world of the cells.
Moreover, the sexual life energy, which had previously been
understood as existing only within living organisms, was now seen
as continuous with an omnipresent orgone energy enveloping
the earth.

Unidentified Flying Objects

Our last example of the thematic structure we have been
pursuing concerns Reich's reactions to the phenomenon of
unidentified flying objects. During the early 1950's he began to
imagine that UFO's, then being reported in fairly large numbers,
were space machines piloted by intelligent beings from other
planets. He thought of these beings as having benevolent intentions
toward humanity, but he also entertained the possibility that they
might be responsible for the severe droughts which were
experienced in America during 1952 and 1953.

> In this case let us not fool ourselves: the war between earth and
> an invading enemy from space using weapons strange to us is
> already on and must be met *right away*. We must permit
> ourselves to think of war as a silent, unnoticed, slow-working
> but deliberate destruction of life...[quoted in Boadella 1974,
> p. 302].

Reich's ideas about the space machines are recalled in the
autobiographical fragment, *A Book of Dreams* (1974) by his son,
Peter. According to this source, Reich was eventually persuaded
that a cosmic war was actually in progress and that he and his son
were the first human beings to engage the hostile space-machines in
battle. The weapon used to defend the earth was the "space gun,"
an adaptation of a device which had been applied in earlier
attempts to influence cloud formation and modify the weather.

The space gun was an arrangement of hollow pipes designed to drain off orgone energy from any object at which it was aimed. It provided a means for disabling the invaders because Reich believed their ships were powered by orgone energy. The aliens' purposes were obscure, but he thought their presence was "killing the sky," dehydrating the atmosphere, and contributing to the formation of deserts.

This fantasy of heroic space war, remote though it may seem from the ideas and projects we have already described, actually represents a transposition into physical planetary terms of Reich's obsessive concern with the suppression of life. He had begun to think of the earth and its atmosphere as functionally analogous to a living organism. By virtue of the earth's dependence on the free streaming of orgone in the sky, it was also vulnerable to energy-depleting death forces, this time personified in the image of alien beings riding in spaceships; and just as Reich had earlier made efforts to rid the world of character armor, mental illness, fascism and cancer, now he defended humanity against the assault from outer space.

A PIVOTAL CHILDHOOD TRAUMA

The purpose of the first part of this chapter was to demonstrate the relentlessness with which Reich conducted his messianic defense of life. Let us now turn to the psychological background of his extraordinary career. The following account is based on the information provided in the biography written by his third wife, Ilse Ollendorff Reich (1970).

Reich's family circle during his childhood years included himself, his mother and father, and his brother, Robert, who was three years younger. They lived on a farm in Austria where Wilhelm and Robert received their educations from a series of private tutors. During the years of his early childhood Reich had no friends outside of his family, and he spent most of his time playing by himself. The father is said to have been a brutal authoritarian man, given to violent outbursts of temper, but very much in love with his wife and extremely jealous of other men's interests in her. The mother was an attractive but reportedly rather unintelligent person who, for the most part, remained subdued by her more dominant husband. Reich loved his mother and throughout his childhood was always competing with his brother for her exclusive affection. He had wanted a sister originally, and when first informed of the birth of a brother, he said he was not interested and that they could take the new baby back. Both brothers claimed to be the favorite of their family cook, and they were constantly trying to outdo one another in riding, hunting, and other activities. According to Ilse Ollendorff Reich,

> Both brothers seemed to have acquired the father's tendency toward violent temper outbursts, and one would often react to such outbursts in the other with the remark "you behave like father," which came close to being an insult [1970, p. 24].

Reich was just fourteen years old when he underwent what was surely the most profound psychological trauma of his entire life. He discovered his mother was having a secret love affair with one of his tutors, and probably reacting with deep disappointment, anger, and moral condemnations, he reported his mother's infidelity to his father. She responded by killing herself. The catastrophic suicide of Reich's mother appears to have been the direct outcome of his own actions. Ilse Ollendorff Reich describes the situation as follows:

> There seems to be little doubt from what I could gather in my talks with Reich, his family, and some close friends that he played a role in his mother's death by revealing her love affair with one of the tutors to his father...Reich was unable to resolve this question...there were certain problems he was never able to face [p. 25].

Although nothing is known directly about Reich's immediate reactions to the loss of his mother, we believe the circumstances of her death constituted the nuclear situation around which the structure of his representational world crystallized. The probable impact of this childhood tragedy can be constructed by reference to the subsequent course of his life. If it is assumed that in betraying his mother's unfaithfulness the young Reich was acting out of an identification with his father's authoritarian and sexually restrictive values, then the reasons for his subsequent life of struggle against sexual repression begin to become clear. Since in acting on the basis of a narrow code of sexual morality he was responsible for the death of the one person he loved above all others, an immense burden of pain and guilt must have been generated. What could be a better way to atone for his fateful act of betrayal than devoting himself to the eradication of all those values and ways of thinking which had motivated him? This line of reasoning also sheds light on why he regarded the repression of sexuality as such a vicious and deadly force in human affairs. This was because his own attempt to inhibit his beloved mother's sexuality led directly to her suicide.

Reich idealized his mother after her death; in later years he is reported to have spoken of her only in the most glowing and positive of terms. His attitude toward his father, by contrast, appears to have become deeply negative. He rarely if ever spoke of him, implied on several occasions that he was not really his father's son, and eventually even went so far as to suggest that he was the offspring of his mother's relationship with a man from outer space (I.O. Reich 1970). Such fantasies underline the degree to which he wished to dissociate himself from everything his father represented (especially authoritarianism and sexually repressive morality).

Reich's conscious idealization of the image of his dead mother seems to have involved the splitting off and repression of the disappointing and enraging qualities she had displayed by being unfaithful to her marriage. Nevertheless, during his adult life he was continually plagued by the problem of sexual jealousy. In commenting on the experience of being his wife, Ilse Ollendorff Reich makes the following interesting observations.

Always, in times of stress, one of Reich's very human failings came to the foreground, and that was his violent jealousy. He would always emphatically deny that he was jealous, but there is no getting away from the fact that he would accuse his wife of infidelity with any man who came to his mind as a possible rival, whether colleague, friend, local shopkeeper, or casual acquaintance. It was one of those strange contradictions in Reich's makeup, and one that must have been founded on some basic unresolved feelings of insecurity, because there were in fact no reasons for these jealousies [1970, p. 71].

This irrational behavior is all the more remarkable in view of Reich's repeated insistence in his writings that strictly enforced monogamous relationships are contrary to the sexual needs and emotional health of human beings. Apparently, his conscious idealization of his mother and of sexual freedom was not sufficiently strong to prevent the periodic return of the split-off image of the treacherous unfaithful mother who had disappointed him by committing adultery.

The anti-sexual death forces envisioned by Reichian theory (whether they are localized in the armor, fascism, T-bacilli, or invading space machines) can now be seen to correspond to an aspect of Reich's own personality. This was the side of him which was closely identified with his father and which reacted to his mother's unfaithfulness with anger, moral indignation, and betrayal. The sexual life energies (in the biological core, the blue PA bions, and the omnipresent orgone), on the other hand, correspond to and derive from the reactively idealized image of his mother. This was the mother whom he had loved and whose death he had experienced as a shattering loss for which he blamed himself. Viewing the evolution of his work in these terms, we might interpret his relentless struggle against the death forces as a sustained attempt to undo his act of betrayal and thereby magically restore his mother to life. Hence, Reich's central theoretical reifications, in which the dialectical struggle between anti-sexual death forces and the sexual life energies becomes the dominant metapsychological (and ultimately metaphysical) principle governing human existence, can be viewed as a symbolic crystallization of his lifelong personal quest for absolution from guilt and for the resurrection of his beloved mother.

FURTHER ASPECTS OF REICH'S LIFE AND THOUGHT

Now that our major hypotheses concerning Reich's personal history have been given, we shall turn to certain other aspects of his experiences and try to deepen our understanding of his life and work. Anyone who reads his works chronologically cannot escape the impression that his psychological condition was deteriorating over the course of his last twenty years. There was no specific point in time when he became psychotic; the delusional beliefs of his last years were the culmination of a progressively advancing decompensation process which already began to show itself in his first biological studies. In the course of this deterioration his metapsychological reifications proliferated into an all-encompassing delusional reconstruction of reality.

It appears that the disastrous course of Reich's relationship with Freud and the psychoanalytic movement played a large part in determining his ultimate fate. He had originally idolized Freud, describing himself as a "worshipful disciple" and as having "unlimited devotion" to psychoanalysis. The major factor he reports which contributed to his disappointment and break with Freud concerns his interests in politics and the reform of society. As we stated earlier, Reich became disillusioned with individual treatment during the late 1920s and began to believe that psychoanalysis should ally itself with Marxist sociology and seek to completely alter the structure of social life. In an interview about his relationship with Freud, he recalled Freud's response to these ideas:

> Your standpoint has nothing to do with psychoanalysis....It is not our purpose, or the purpose of our existence, to save the world [Higgins and Raphael 1968, p. 52].

Ilse Ollendorff Reich argues that these disagreements over the social implications and responsibilities of psychoanalysis were not the only reasons for the break. According to her, Freud refused to take Reich for a personal analysis, and this refusal was experienced as an intolerable rejection. In any case, the difficulties with Freud signalled the beginning of a series of professional controversies which resulted in Reich's expulsion from the International Psychoanalytic Association in 1934. The movement to which he had given unlimited devotion and whose leader he had worshipped, had disowned him and dissociated itself from him. Reich describes his reactions to this humiliation as follows:

whatever happened between the International Psychoanalytic Association and myself, I ascribed, at first, to this person or that person, to the psychoanalytic association, to a betrayal of Freud and psychoanalysis, etc. And all that turned out to be wrong.... What happened at that time not only happened in the IPA from 1926 to 1934. It has happened all through the ages. It happened in the Christian Church fifteen hundred years ago. It happened in every home on this planet... [Higgins and Raphael 1968, pp. 6–7].

What Reich is referring to is the unending human suppression of life. These images of betrayal and life suppression suggest that in being expelled from the psychoanalytic movement, he re-experienced the tragedy of his mother's death. Let us now turn to some of Reich's later writings and study the continuing manifestations of his personal struggle. It is a testimony to the constancy of human personality that even as his psychological state deteriorated and his thought became increasingly grandiose, the essential structure of his ideas remained the same.

Images of History, Civilization, and Nature

In the *Quest of the Historical Jesus* (1906) Albert Schweitzer comments that nowhere is an individual's personality more clearly revealed than in his interpretation of the figure of Jesus Christ. This comment seems to hold especially well for Reich, who saw in Jesus a personification of the natural and undistorted essence of the life process. His book, *The Murder of Christ* (1953), uses the story of Jesus as an allegory for the chronic relentless destruction of life and sexuality which Reich believed characterized the whole of human civilization. The history of man is here presented as an "emotional plague" of misery and pain; without being aware of it, human beings are trapped in this plague by the scourge of the character armor. All those persons living within the trap, on account of their devastated emotional condition and armored incapacity to live fully and naturally, become murderously angry toward anyone who seeks to restore life to its true and uninhibited state. Reich interprets the crucifixion of Christ in these terms:

Let us subsume all manifestations of this hatred against the living under the heading "Murder of Christ".... The secret of why Jesus Christ had to die still stands unsolved. We shall experience this tragedy of two thousand years ago, which had such tremendous effects on the destiny of mankind, as a logical necessity within the domain of armored man.... The murder of Christ represents a riddle which harassed human existence at least over the whole period of written history. It is the problem of the *armored* human character structure, and not of Christ alone. Christ became a victim of this human character structure because he had developed the qualities and manners of conduct which act upon the armored character structure like red color on the emotional system of a wild bull. Thus we may say that *Christ presents the principle of Life per se* [pp. 5-6].

This image of Christ, by virtue of its being a symbol of all that is natural, good and pure about life, belongs to that class of Reichian concepts which we earlier argued were derivatives of the idealized image of his mother (the biological core, the orgone, etc.). We can thus read the above passage autobiographically, in which case the tragic effect of Christ's crucifixion on the destiny of mankind becomes a symbol of the shattering trauma experienced by Reich when his mother killed herself. In this light it is interesting to read his comments on Judas Iscariot, who betrayed Jesus just as Reich had betrayed his mother.

[Judas Iscariot] is the child beaten down into the mud, grown up to be a traitor by structure.... He will feel like a dirty rat but he will not have the courage to kill himself [1953, p. 89].

In *Ether, God and Devil* (1949), Reich had developed images of history and civilization which mirror the concerns of his personal existence in a substantially similar way. Again presenting the history of mankind as an insane chaos of suffering and murder, he describes the human tendency to seek out scapegoats who can be blamed and found guilty for the misery and destruction of life. One of the great errors into which human thought falls, according to his argument, is just this blaming of someone or something external for the problems which actually stem from within man's character structure and from within his own damaged organism.

> It is only by keeping strictly outside this inferno that one can be amazed that the human animal continued to shriek "Guilty!" without doubting its own sanity, without even once asking about the origin of this guilt.... Only human beings who are forced to hide something catastrophic are capable of erring so consistently [1949, p. 30].

The catastrophic reality being hidden was a dimly felt degeneracy, a deviation from nature; in short, the armoring of bio-sexual impulses. Reich defines himself here as outside the "inferno" of human error. This means that he also imagined himself as outside the trap of the armored character structure, that is to say, as a Christ-like defender of "the principle of Life *per se.*" His late writings carry the unmistakable implication that virtually everyone in the world, except for himself, was plagued by the deadly armor. These thoughts express a projection on to humanity of his own most central conflict. The biological armoring which he held responsible for the disastrous course of human history (and which was therefore his "scapegoat") corresponds to the moral condemnations, jealousy and hatefulness which were originally split off from his self-representation under the impact of his mother's suicide. As seems to be the case with all messianic salvation fantasies (Stolorow and Atwood 1973, Atwood 1978), Reich's struggle to lead man out of the trap was an attempt to save the world from the problem with which he himself was afflicted.

Further symbols of this splitting process found their way into his writings on physical nature. It will be recalled that the concept of the orgone posits the existence of an omnipresent creative energy which regulates psychological, biological and physical phenomena. As described in *Cosmic Superimposition* (1949), orgone energy envelops the earth and is distributed throughout space; galaxies are formed from its streamings, it holds the planets in their orbits, and life itself is generated out of its smaller-scale concentrations in non-living matter. At the same time, the creative dynamism of the orgone is disturbed—another force, which Reich called deadly orgone energy (DOR), is also at work in the world. He thought of DOR as "stalemated" orgone and as having deadly effects on all living things. Reich "observed" the two types of energy in the atmosphere and speculated that their interactions accounted for the origin of whirlwinds, tornadoes and related meteorological phenomena.

> ...the principle of sequestration of the invading distur-ber...holds true...in the formation of dust devils, tornadoes, and similar disturbances of the atmosphere. DOR clouds are encircled by highly excited OR [orgone] energy.... It is as if the. atmosphere were feverish ... the principle is clear: sequestration and elimination of the stale intruder ... [1961, p. 453].

The orgone in the atmosphere reacts to the presence of deadly orgone energy by surrounding and sequestering it into isolated pockets. The purity of the unaffected air is thereby safeguarded and preserved. These images of the feverish sequestering off of a deadly stale intruder vividly symbolize the splitting process on which Reich's life foundered; namely, the splitting off and repression of the image of his disappointing and sexually treacherous mother in order to preserve her as an idealized object, and the splitting off and sequestering of his own disappointment, jealous rage, and moral indignation in order to preserve the image of an idealized, messianic self.

Reich emigrated from Europe in 1939 and spent most of the last period of his life at his institute in Rangely, Maine. These were the years during which his concern with the problem of sexuality underwent its final expansion into the all-embracing world-system known as cosmic orgone biophysics. This was also the period when his use of the orgone energy accumulator in the treatment of cancer became the subject of a lengthy investigation by the Food and Drug Administration, an investigation which in 1957 culminated in his arrest and imprisonment. It is perhaps not surprising that Reich submitted to the loss of his liberty as an act of holy martyrdom. In a letter to his son Peter only a few months before his fatal heart attack in prison, he wrote:

> My present predicament is an *honor*....I am proud to be in the company of Socrates, Christ, Bruno, Galileo....You know and have learned to trust in God as we have understood the *universal existence and rule of Life and Love* [I.O. Reich 1970, p. 195].

What more fitting way to find a final absolution for his tragic role in his mother's death than to end his life as a martyr to the cause of Life and Love?

SUMMARY AND CONCLUSIONS

This chapter has examined the relationship between Wilhelm Reich's life history and the evolution of his scientific work, and is offered as a case in point of the subjectivity of personality theory. Reich's essential contribution, in our view, lies in his formulations of character defenses, i.e., the multiple ways in which a person's solutions to nuclear crises and conflicts may become frozen into static configurations of experience, rigid patterns of conduct, and quasi-permanent muscular and postural tensions. His intellectual system taken as a whole is a network of ideas and images which was profoundly affected by the tragedy of his personal existence. We have seen how the considerable powers of observation and inference displayed in his early work on character analysis were gradually eroded by his messianic need to save the world. We have also seen the probable origin of his obsession with the defense of life and sexuality in the childhood circumstances of his mother's suicide.

REFERENCES

Atwood, G. (1978). On the origin and dynamics of messianic salvation fantasies. *International Review of Psycho-Analysis* 5(1):85–96.

Boadella, D. (1974). *Wilhelm Reich: The Evolution of His Work.* Chicago: Henry Regnery.

Higgins, M., and Raphael, C. (1968). *Reich Speaks of Freud.* New York: Noonday Press.

Reich, I.O. (1970). *Wilhelm Reich: A Personal Biography.* New York: Avon Books.

Reich, P. (1974). *A Book of Dreams.* Greenwich, Conn.: Fawcett Publications.

Reich, W. (1932). The imposition of sexual morality. In *Sex-Pol: Essays, 1929–1934,* ed. Lee Baxandall, pp. 89–249. New York: Vintage Books, 1972.

———(1933a). *Character Analysis.* New York: Noonday Press, 1949.

———(1933b). *The Mass Psychology of Fascism.* New York: Farrar, Straus and Giroux, 1973.

———(1942a). *The Function of the Orgasm.* New York: World Publishing Co., 1971.

———(1942b). The carcinomatous shrinking biopathy. In *Wilhelm Reich: Selected Writings,* pp. 228–271. New York: Noonday Press, 1961.

———(1948). *The Cancer Biopathy.* New York: Farrar, Straus and Giroux, 1973.

———(1949). *Ether, God and Devil/ Cosmic Superimposition.* New York: Farrar, Straus and Giroux, 1973.

———(1952). Cosmic orgone engineering. In *Wilhelm Reich: Selected Writings,* pp. 433–466. New York: Noonday Press, 1961.

———(1953). *The Murder of Christ.* New York: Simon and Schuster.

Rycroft, C. (1969). *Wilhelm Reich.* New York: Viking Press.

Schweitzer, A. (1906). *Quest of the Historical Jesus.* New York: Macmillan, 1968.

Stolorow, R., and Atwood, G. (1973). Messianic projects and early object relations. *American Journal of Psychoanalysis* 33:213–214.

Wyckoff, J. (1973). *Wilhelm Reich: Life Force Explorer.* Greenwich, Conn.: Fawcett Publications.

CHAPTER 5

Otto Rank

In recent years the problem of narcissism has increasingly moved into the limelight of psychoanalytic investigation. This is evidenced, for example, by the large number of articles on the subject appearing in psychoanalytic publications, and by the fact that in a recent poll Kohut's (1971) work on narcissism was rated among the most meaningful contributions to contemporary psychoanalysis (Goldberg 1974). The reasons for the current psychoanalytic focus on narcissism are at least twofold. First, advances in psychoanalytic understanding over the past twenty years or so have given analysts the conceptual and technical tools to deal effectively with the problems of narcissism and the narcissistic disturbances (Stolorow 1975a). And secondly, the contemporary exposure of Western man to a radical deterioration and breakdown of collective (social-structural, cultural, religious) supports for his sense of existing as a significant self has in our time made the struggle for selfhood (which lies at the heart of the phenomenon of narcissism) much more of an individual problem than was the case in earlier historical periods.

In this context, Otto Rank,[1] who anticipated the breakdown of collective supports for the sense of self (*AA*), emerges as a fascinating figure in the history of psychoanalysis. Rank immersed himself in the study of "narcissism themes" decades before the problem of narcissism began to dominate the psychoanalytic literature. In this chapter we shall first document Rank's precocious understanding of narcissism and, in particular, certain of his theoretical formulations which prefigured recent advances in this area. Secondly, we shall attempt to locate some of the sources of Rank's interest in and understanding of narcissism within his subjective experiences and life history.

RANK'S WORK

The Birth Trauma

We shall begin with a discussion of *The Trauma of Birth* (1924), since it was this rather notorious work that marked both the blossoming of Rank's originality and his severance from the Freudian inner circle. Rank claims in this work to "recognize in the birth trauma the ultimate biological basis of the psychical." Beginning with certain observations of separation anxiety within the analytic transference, he concludes that the primal anxiety at birth forms the basis of every anxiety or fear, and that every pleasure has as its final aim the reestablishment of the primal pleasure of the intrauterine state. He further insists that "the whole circle of human creation," including all neurotic and psychotic symptoms, dreams, fantasies, myths, religion, art, philosophy, revolutions and wars, ultimately represent attempts to materialize the "lost paradise" of the intrauterine state and/or repetitions of the birth trauma.

In another context (*PS*), Rank cogently argues that imagery pertaining to biological events can often be interpreted as "concretions," i.e., as representations of psychological processes by concrete biological symbols. Such an interpretation may be applied to the theme of the birth trauma as it appeared in his own writings, for it seems abundantly clear in the light of his later preoccupation with the problem of individuation (*WT*), that Rank used the birth trauma theme as a concrete biological symbol for the often painful psychological process of self-differentiation and self-articulation. A passage from one of Rank's youthful "Daybooks" which we find in Taft's biography (1958) suggests that as early as age twenty he self-consciously used birth imagery to give symbolic representation to his own difficulties and achievements in self-object differentiation:

> If the world is my projection, so is becoming conscious of this projection my birth [Taft 1958, p. 41].

In *Will Therapy* (1926), Rank cautions, almost as an aside, that the birth trauma theme should not be taken literally, but rather as a "universal symbol of the ego's discovery of itself and its separation" from the mother and mother surrogates. And in his theoretical synthesis, *Truth and Reality* (1931), Rank is concerned much more with the birth of individuality than with the biological event of birth.

In terms of the representational world, the birth trauma theme in Rank's writings appears as a concrete biological symbol of the developmental process of consolidating a bounded self-representation which is differentiated from primary object representations. Similarly, the theme of the regressively longed for intrauterine state concretely symbolizes the "lost paradise" of the primitive undifferentiated symbiotic state in which self- and object-representations are merged. That Rank places such emphasis on the psychological processes and representational configurations (albeit in the guise of concrete biological symbols) which lie at the heart of the problem of narcissism, alludes already to his insights into other narcissism themes.

In *The Trauma of Birth* Rank posits the aim of psychoanalytic therapy as detachment from the primal mother fixation through "a repetition of the birth trauma, with the help of an experienced midwife." To this end he recommends that the therapist allow the patient a "far-reaching restoration of the primal situation," followed by a phase of working through the process of "severance from the substitute object" (the analyst). Here Rank appears to be describing, again in biological metaphor, the establishment and dissolution of what would currently be called a narcissistic transference. Although many of his technical recommendations (such as premature and arbitrary end-setting and a therapeutic obsession with the termination process) are of doubtful value, the use Rank made of the patient's reaction to the ending of each analytic hour is reminiscent of the necessity in the treatment of narcissistic disturbances to pay careful analytic attention to all such disruptions of the narcissistic transference (Kohut 1971). Similarly, Rank's ultimate therapeutic goal for the patient, to "supplement a part of his development which was neglected or lacking," calls to mind the therapeutic goal in the treatment of certain narcissistic disturbances—growth in the patient's tenuous capacity for autonomous self-esteem regulation through the continuation and completion of a developmental process that became arrested before the achievement of separation-individuation (Mahler, Pine and Bergman 1975) and consolidation of a cohesive and bounded self-representation (Kohut 1971).

A number of authors (Jacobson 1964, Kohut 1971, Mahler, Pine and Bergman 1975) have noted that developmentally the blissful primitive symbiotic state (so-called "primary narcissism") is inevitably disturbed by the shortcomings of maternal care. Kohut (1971) has argued that the child attempts to replace the lost perfection of the symbiotic dyad along two pathways: "(a) by establishing a grandiose and exhibitionistic image of the self: *the grandiose self*; and (b) by giving over the previous perfection to an admired, omnipotent (transitional) self-object: *the idealized parent imago*" (p. 25). As we shall see, much of Rank's theorizing directly or indirectly touches on various transformations and symbolizations of these two archaic narcissistic configurations which play such an important role in the narcissistic disturbances.

The Hero

Rank's interest in and intuitive understanding of the vicissitudes of infantile idealizations of the self and of the object world can be detected in his early work in applied psychoanalysis, *The Myth of the Birth of the Hero* (1909). Noting the parallels between heroic myths and certain wishful fantasies of childhood, Rank interprets the common theme of the hero's secret descent from noble parents as a collective version of the "family romance" of the individual child, in which the actual parents are denied and replaced by "exalted personages" of a higher status. Rank understood such fantasies to be a reaction of the child to the inevitable disappointments and disillusionment with his actual parents and "the expression of the child's longing for the vanished happy time, when his father still appeared to be the strongest and greatest man, and the mother seemed the dearest and most beautiful woman.... Thus the overvaluation of the earliest years of childhood again claims its own in these fancies" (p. 71).

As this indicates his understanding of the child's creation of idealized object imagos, so another passage points to Rank's insight into a common sequence later also described by Kohut (1971), in which traumatic disappointment by the idealized parents impels the child to regressively recoil into fantasy images of the grandiose self:

> The entire family romance in general owes its origin to the feeling of being neglected—namely, the assumed hostility of the parents. In the myth, this hostility goes so far that the parents refuse to let the child be born.... The overcoming of all these obstacles also expresses the idea that the future hero has actually overcome the greatest difficulties by virtue of his birth, for he has victoriously thwarted all attempts to prevent it [p. 76].

Rank also recognizes the grandiose-narcissistic components of the oedipal constellation as symbolized in heroic myth:

> The true hero of the romance is, therefore, the ego, which finds itself in the hero, by reverting to the time when the ego was itself a hero, through its first heroic act, i.e., the revolt against the father [p. 84].

Even the incest motif is interpreted in terms of its grandiose-narcissistic aspect, as an expression of the wish to be born again as one's own son, but into a more exalted station.

And finally, Rank gives an intriguing account of the primitive mechanisms of self- and object-splitting, so common in the narcissistic disturbances (Kernberg 1975), which can result in the creation of "doubles"—i.e., series of duplications of self- and object-representations. These operations are all in the service of "the exalting tendency that is inherent in the family romance. The hero, in the various duplications of himself and his parents, ascends the social scale…" (p. 88).

Rank, then, in this early work (*The Myth of the Birth of the Hero*), presents a precocious account of the processes of narcissistic reparation and restitution which occur along the pathways mapped out by the two archaic narcissistic configurations, the idealized parent imago and the grandiose self.

The Double

In *The Double* (1914), in many ways his most fascinating work, Rank addresses himself directly to the "problems of man's relation to himself—and the fateful disturbance of this relation," i.e., to the problems of narcissism and the narcissistic disturbances. To that end he presents a detailed analysis of the theme of the "uncanny double" or "second self" as it appears in both modern Western literature and primitive myth and superstition in such guises as the mirror image, the shadow, the portrait, the twin, the dual personality, the apparition, the guardian spirit, and the immortal soul. In the course of his analysis he alludes to or explicitly elaborates rich insights into issues which are central to an understanding of the narcissistic disorders: the interference of narcissistic conflicts with the ability to love; the dread of self-dissolution as manifested in the terror of confronting and/or losing one's mirror image; the fear of sexual love as a threat to self-integrity; the problem of mortification, self-hatred and the need for narcissistic repair; the interconnections between disturbed self-representation, depersonalization, hypochondriasis and paranoia;

the importance of splitting, projective and introjective processes in narcissistic disorders; etc.

A central idea in *The Double* is the connection between the morbid dread of death and primitive or pathological narcissism. Rank clearly recognizes that (from the point of view of the grandiose self) death, the final eradication of the self, is the ultimate narcissistic injury (see Stolorow 1974). Hence, the wish to remain forever young and the fear of becoming old relate to "one of the deepest problems of the self." Rank notes that to narcissistic personalities "the expectation of the unavoidable destiny of death is unbearable," and that suicide may be for them a voluntary seeking of death in order to be free of an "intolerable thanatophobia." Rank arrives next at what for him is the deepest meaning of the theme of the double in its varied guises: the narcissistic individual (the child, the primitive, the narcissistically disturbed adult) projects a duplicate representation of the self as a denial of the inevitability of death and an assurance against self-loss.

Rank presents the theme of the double as a materialization of the grandiose (omnipotent, indestructible, immortal) wishful self. It is not surprising, then, that variations on the double theme (the mirror image, the twin) have recently been noted as important components in the narcissistic transference relationships established by narcissistically disturbed patients (see Kohut 1971, for his discussion of the mirror transference and alter-ego or twinship transference).

Although Rank is still working within the libido theory, it would seem to us that in *The Double* he moves somewhat away from a purely economic concept of narcissism and in the direction of a functional conception of narcissism (Stolorow 1975a). He regards both exaggerated self-love and illusory self-duplication as reparative and restitutive reactions to injurious experiences which threaten the self-representation with "damage," "impairment," "immolation" and "dissolution." Interestingly, in his chapter, "Biography as a Background to Literature," he documents the fact that those authors in whose work the double appears as a major theme suffer from a variety of pathological manifestations indicative of severe vulnerability and disturbance in the self-representation. We shall demonstrate that the same holds true for

Rank, for whom the double remained a major theoretical preoccupation throughout his life (*PS, BP*).

The Will

In *Will Therapy* (1926) and *Truth and Reality* (1931), Rank synthesizes his theoretical conceptions of the dynamics of personality and the therapeutic process into a comprehensive "will psychology." The theme of the will, which constitutes Rank's central metapsychological reification, is a highly complicated theoretical construct with multiple, often incompatible meanings and usages. For instance, in the early pages of *Will Therapy* Rank often equates the will with a more or less healthy striving for separation-individuation, independence and personal freedom. Within this usage, the neurotic is described as suffering from a denial of will, brought about by the circumstance that his efforts at separation-individuation generate excessive feelings of anxiety and guilt. The analytic transference situation is regarded as a materialization of the patient's "will conflict"—a conflict between his strivings for separation-individuation (assertion of his own will) and his regressive tendencies to submit to the will of the therapist, experienced as an idealized object. Such a formulation leads Rank to value the patient's "resistance" as an expression of will (striving for separation-individuation). He posits the goal of treatment as the "rehabilitation of will" by working through the "will conflict" and its attendant individuation guilt and separation anxiety in the transference, thus permitting the patient to free himself from the parental imagos and to affirm his own difference and unique individuality. Thus, the goal of strengthening the patient's will is equated with the unfolding of "the individual himself, as a separate, different, independent being," "a self-reliant individual, different and differentiated from others," such that the patient "actually feels himself as real."

In these passages, the will is equated with strivings for separation-individuation. But elsewhere, and in contrast to this meaning, the will embodies various derivatives of the archaic grandiose self. In *Will Therapy*, for instance, Rank refers to therapy as a "battle for supremacy," "a great duel of wills" which the patient must win "by the actual overcoming of the therapist and complete ruling of the analytic moment"—a formulation which alludes to the dominance of the grandiose self in both patient and therapist (see Stolorow 1970). Similarly, when Rank enjoins that the therapist "must serve the creative will of the patient as material," and place "the ego of the patient, as will, in the center of the analytic situation," so that the therapist "sinks to the level of assistant ego" of whom "the patient only makes use," he describes the establishment of a transference situation in which the therapist merely mirrors back reflections of the patient's grandiose self (here the will) and accepts the humble role of an impersonal function which the patient cannot perform by himself (Kohut 1971).

The equation of the will with the grandiose self is also contained in Rank's definition of neurosis as a "self-willed overvaluation of self" such that "age, illness and death cannot be accepted." The neurotic "cannot really accept the self as given" and accordingly is compelled to "remodel it in terms of his own will," "to create himself in the exact image of his own ideal."

Another passage in *Will Therapy*, which also embodies the grandiose-self meaning of the will, further suggests Rank's insight into the contribution of grandiose wishes to certain forms of moral masochism (see Stolorow 1975b):

[The neurotic] seeks to subject death, this original symbol of the "must," to his will, and, as it were, at his own instigation transforms the death punishment which is placed upon life into a lifelong punishment which he imposes upon himself [p. 127].

In *Truth and Reality*, the grandiose-self meaning of the will is even more strongly affirmed. Here Rank interprets the concept of a creative, omnipotent, omniscient God as a projective personification of the individual will. The will becomes a "self-deifying tendency," equated with an individual's "presumption in wanting to be not only omniscient like God, but to be God himself." Describing what would currently be called narcissistic transferences, Rank asserts that "the therapeutic value of the analytic situation lies in the fact that it affords the individual an unreal solution of his will conflict corresponding to the creation of God from the [his] own will" (p. 288). Here, indeed, the will is grandiose.

And finally, in his psychological-anthropological study, *Psychology and the Soul* (1930), Rank equates the will with the grandiose quest for personal indestructibility and immortality:

> We shall consider the uncompromising tendencies toward immortality in his [the patient's] dreams, his living, and his works, all as phenomena of will [p. 37].

The belief in the soul (and hence in immortality) provides "proof that the individual will is God even over death." Ideologies of immortality are manifestations of the "omnipotence of will which seems...to stand outside the natural order and within that of the supernatural."

We have documented that Rank, in his separate descriptions of the will, fuses the healthy striving for separation-individuation with images of the primitive, grandiose, omnipotent, omniscient, indestructible, wishful self. Hence, Rank confuses and confounds the *process* of separation-individuation with certain manifestations of a *pathological failure* to achieve separation-individuation (i.e., with a developmentally arrested representational world which remains organized around visions of the archaic grandiose self). This confusion and confounding may be one basis for the lack of acceptance of Rank's "will psychology" and reflect Rank's own difficulties in the narcissistic realm.

Narcissistic Love

Rank recognized and emphasized the narcissistic components in a wide variety of "love" relationships. We shall first make note of his analyses of three specific love situations (homosexual boy-love, parental love for the child, and oedipal love for the mother), and then consider his more general discussions of the state of being in love.

Rank views homosexual boy-love, typified in ancient Greek culture, as a purely narcissistic object choice in which the individual seeks self-glorification and self-perpetuation through an attachment to a love object who personifies his own idealized, wishful self:

> the adult sought to impress his self, his own spirit, his real soul upon the beloved youth. In this phenomenon there lies the deep relationship of so-called homosexuality to narcissism.... In boy-love, man fertilized both spiritually and otherwise the living image of his own soul, which seemed materialized in an ego as idealized and as much like his own body as was possible.... [*PS*, p. 43]

Homosexual boy-love, which is also a variation on the theme of the double, is thus seen as a narcissistic object relationship of the "twinship" or "alter-ego" type (Kohut 1971), in the service of materializing and sustaining the wishful representation of a grandiose, perfectionistic and eternally youthful self. Parental love for the child, according to Rank, is essentially in the same service. In his child the parent finds and loves the embodiment of his own idealized self and the vehicle for his own self-perpetuation (*PS*). Through procreation the parent becomes a "hero immortalized in his children" (*BP*). Indeed, the eternal problem of intergenerational strife is viewed in part as arising from the desperate struggle of the child to protect his own individuality and integrity from being "engulfed" by the "all-devouring" narcissistic claims of the parent for a spiritual successor or double (*ME*).

Even oedipal love is interpreted by Rank as essentially a narcissistic formation in the service of sustaining the grandiose self. At the core of the boy's wish for incest with the mother, according to Rank, is the striving for self-perpetuation, the desire "to be one's own successor," "to beget himself, as it were, as his mother's son and be reborn by her," thus insuring his personal immortality (*BP*).

Rank views not only these varieties of love but also the state of being in love as essentially a manifestation of narcissistic strivings. In *Will Therapy*, for instance, he describes both transference love and the state of being in love in general as basically a narcissistic transference situation:

I consider the transference and the "being in love" which lies at
its root as a projection phenomenon, that is... an attempt of
the individual to personify his own will [grandiose self] in the
other and so to justify it.... "Being in love" is the continuation
of the unreal will justification in God, through the earthly
deification of a real person.... In this voluntary dependence
and subjection of the individual who makes a God for himself
as he yields himself to the deified loved one, we see before us
the... approbation and justification of the own will through
another [p. 60].

[The beloved,] as an object of admiration, adoration, or
veneration, symbolizes the own ego personified, just like God
except that God remains unreal....

[In the beloved] the formerly unreal God image is here
realized; that is, is represented in an actual person who
corresponds to this divine ideal of self... [pp. 61–62].

Furthermore, the individual's will (here the grandiose self) is
justified, fulfilled, sustained, and made good through the approval
of the deified love object. Hence, through the beloved the
individual seeks the "ideal completion of his own ego."

Clearly, then, Rank, in these passages, views the love
relationship as a complex mixture of narcissistic transference
manifestations in which the love object primarily functions to
regulate the self-representation by serving alternately as an
idealized object, as a duplication of the grandiose wishful self, and
as a mirroring, echoing, approving presence. Rank's later analyses
of love also emphasize these varieties of narcissistic transference
manifestations. In *Psychology and the Soul* (1930), for instance,
Rank refers to the love relationship as "the mental mirroring of
ourselves in others, and of them in us." The love object functions as
a personification of the individual's "better, eternal and 'beautiful'
soul." In *Beyond Psychology* (1941) Rank emphasizes the self-
esteem regulating function of the love relationship, in which the
individual "wants to be constantly *made* good through being
loved" by an idealized object:

Modern love is... not a sexual but a psychological problem
experienced in moral terms of good and bad [which] makes

human relationship into a symbiose of two parasites feeding on each other's "goodness" [p. 201].

The individual, by establishing a "symbiotic twinship" with an idealized love object, seeks both "borrowed support" for his self-esteem and self-immortalization through "love for an 'identical' person resembling the self." Rank also recognized that excessive reliance for self-esteem on the love of an idealized object gives rise to the urgent need to please the object who is made the "God-like judge over good and bad," and that this in turn can lead to patterns of total dependency and masochistic surrender, coupled with reactive sadism to protect against self-loss (see Stolorow 1975b).

In *Truth and Reality* Rank incisively identifies the factors that inevitably bring a narcissistic object relationship to grief:

Here, in the love relationship, in the recreation of the other after our own image, we again come up against the real counter-will of the other.... Something is lacking in all real attempts at solution of this will conflict which the unreal God creation...did not have. It is this, the fact that the earthly representatives of the individual ego themselves have an own will and a counter-will against which our own constantly strike....In the love relation which...represents entirely individual creative activity...he runs against the same counter-will which wants to occupy itself creatively on him [pp. 282–288].

This anticipates recent observations in the analysis of narcissistic disorders that a narcissistic transference can be seriously, at times traumatically, disrupted by any circumstance that highlights the actual existence of the object as a real and separate person with needs and wishes of his own (Kohut 1971). Rank, one should note, conceives of the love relationship as a wholly narcissistic affair. In fact, throughout his entire work we could find only meager references to mature object love in which the separate individuality and real qualities of the object are recognized and cherished; at one point Rank indeed questions "how far a true love without idealization and ego assimilation is possible" (*WT*). Consistent with his conception of love, he posits one goal of therapy as the transformation of the love need into ethical ideal formation and self-acceptance (*WT*), a goal which seems appropriate to the resolution of the narcissistic transferences (Kohut 1971), but totally inappropriate with regard to mature object love. Rank's relative neglect of object love and his nearly total emphasis on narcissistic object relationship point once again to his subjective preoccupations within the narcissistic realm.

Sexual Dread and Self-Dissolution

Rank interprets the dread of sexuality not as a derivative of infantile sexual conflict, but rather as an expression of what currently would be termed the individual's narcissistic vulnerability and need to sustain self-integrity. Essentially, Rank argues that the individual ultimately dreads involvement in the sexual act because it poses the threat of "complete loss of self" (*WT*), of "absorption... by another" (*PS*), of "dissolution of the self" (*BP*), and hence is universally equated with the spectre of death (*WT, PS, BP*). The individual dreads sexuality as the expression of a "powerful racial instinct threatening to devour his personality" (*BP*), and withholds himself from all-absorbing sexual experiences for fear of "a complete loss of individuality" (*WT*). The threat posed by sexual involvement is that of disintegration of self-boundaries and fragmentation of the self-representation; in short, narcissistic decompensation. Furthermore, to succumb to the domination of the biologically given "generic sexual compulsion" would be intolerable to the omnipotent will (*TR*)—i.e., would jeopardize the archaic grandiose self.

Sexual conflict and sexual pathology arise, according to Rank, when the individual struggles to preserve self-integrity by attempting to "force the sex instinct into the service of his individual will" (*TR*), i.e., when narcissistic reparative efforts, such as the animation of the grandiose self (will), become primitively sexualized (see Kohut 1971, Stolorow 1975b). Rank views masturbation, for example, as "an ego victory...a successful attempt to put the sexual instinct under the control of the individual will" (*TR*). Similarly, the sexual perversions function to sustain self-cohesion, as "the individual overemphasizes single components... in order not to succumb to the totality of the sexual urge" (*WT*). Through the details of perverse activity the threatened individual achieves the "partialization" which is "necessary for the preservation of individuality, in opposition to the total claim of sexuality" (*WT*).

According to Rank, not only sexuality, but any sort of emotional involvement with, or emotional surrender to, another person is dreaded as posing the threat of self-dissolution and is symbolically equated with death. Hence arises Rank's insight into the self-sustaining and self-restoring function of narcissistic withdrawal and self-absorption:

> it seems as if this concentration on the own ego were only a defense mechanism against the partial giving up of the self, *cement*, as it were, that *holds the parts of the ego together...* [*WT* p. 141; italics added].

To the extent that emotional yielding and involvement with others threatens weakness and a "softening of will" (self-dissolution), narcissistic defenses are mobilized in the service of "will-hardening" (*TR*)—of "ego maintenance" and "ego protection against the partial or total loss of self in the other" (*WT*).

It will at this juncture come as no surprise that a collection of Rank's statements describing the so-called "neurotic type" constitute a quite accurate picture of what currently would be diagnosed as a severe narcissistic personality disorder. The neurotic, as portrayed by Rank, is an individual who is more or less totally occupied with sustaining or restoring his fragile self-representation in the face of the threat of its complete fragmentation and disintegration. The neurotic's pervasive fear of "ego dissolution" and resulting preoccupation with "self-maintenance" make necessary his emotional restraint and "holding back the ego" from emotional involvement with others (*WT*). He "attempts to preserve his own psychical self by cutting himself off from the natural life processes" (*BP*). His efforts to sustain self-cohesion by striving for a hopelessly grandiose-perfectionistic "re-creation of the given self" (*WT*) burden him with tormenting self-consciousness and self-recrimination, and leave him perpetually "wavering between his Godlikeness and his nothingness" (*TR*). Of necessity remaining "ego-bound" and egocentric, the neurotic experiences all events as "alterations of himself" and hence is incapable of "organizing himself as an entity of the world" (*WT*).

Rank essentially equates "neurosis" with "narcissistic disorder." Just as he one-sidedly emphasizes the narcissistic components of love to the virtual neglect of more differentiated attachments, similarly Rank, with great insight but no less one-sidedly emphasizes the narcissistic disturbances to the virtual neglect of psychopathology rooted in emotional conflicts in relation to objects experienced as separate from the self. Not surprisingly, then, Rank's description of the desired outcome of a successful working through process within the therapeutic relationship bears a close resemblance to current formulations of the result of successfully working through the narcissistic transference with a narcissistically disordered patient (Kohut 1971), but at the same time it is of questionable relevance to the treatment of a transference neurosis where non-narcissistic pathology predominates. In *Will Therapy*, for instance, Rank formulates the results of successful therapy as follows:

> [The patient] no longer seeks to assimilate the world to his ego.... The best proof is in the end phase of the therapeutic process where the assistant ego, the role of the therapist hitherto, becomes a real ego; that is, when the loss of the therapist is no longer perceived painfully as ego-loss, but can be accepted as the breaking in of reality to the ego life....[Hence] the therapist has come through and beyond his role of assistant ego into his real meaning... [pp. 178–179].

Thus, the formerly merged self-object (Kohut 1971) becomes subjectively differentiated into two separate persons, "one the therapist, who should become objective reality, and the other, the own ego which should become inner reality..." (*WT* p. 187).

One could scarcely imagine a better description of the consolidation of a differentiated and bounded self-representation and the growth of object constancy, which is the outcome of successfully working through the narcissistic transferences. At the same time, however, such a formulation has as its sole emphasis growth in the narcissistic realm to the virtual neglect of emotional conflicts experienced in relation to differentiated objects.

The Artist

The theme of the artist, a preoccupation throughout Rank's adult life, provided a major focus for his first (*K*) as well as his last (*AA, BP*) published works. This theme is of particular interest on at least two counts. First, Rank conceives of the so-called neurotic type basically as a miscarried artist (*AA*). Hence, Rank's understanding of the artistic personality is intimately linked with his analysis of neurosis. Essentially, in Rank's view, the artist and the neurotic are both driven by the same core narcissistic conflicts. The artistic person is capable of channelizing these conflicts adaptively and partially satisfying his narcissistic needs through creative production. The neurotic, in contrast, is unequal to this task and remains self-absorbed. (See Kohut 1971, on the contribution of narcissistic conflicts to artistic creativeness.)

Secondly, the theme of the artist is of special interest in that Rank clearly identified himself with the artistic type. As his biographer Jessie Taft (1958) observed:

He never doubted for long that he belonged to the group he called "artist," which for him included the philosopher, the poet, the hero, the musical genius, in short all great creative personalities...[p. 271].

And she observes further, and a study of Rank's own life leaves little doubt, that his analysis of the creative personality is largely autobiographical and the result of his own introspection:

Rank's knowledge of both artist and neurosis depended primarily on his own make-up... [p. 275].

Hence, the theme of the artist provides a convenient bridge between our consideration of Rank's theories and the subjective experiences which shaped them.

All of the narcissism themes which we have enumerated are again reanimated in Rank's portrayal of the artistic type. The artist or genius type is forever struggling to separate himself from the collectivity and liberate himself from the prevailing ideology, and through his creative production achieve his own "self-begetting" and "self-rebirth" (*AA*). The artist's own self-created individuated self is his first creative work and throughout his life "remains fundamentally his chief work" (*AA*). The true artistic type "may be thought of as the hero's spiritual double" (*BP*). The "creator-impulse" is the embodiment par excellence of the omnipotent will, the "will-to-self-immortalization," which strives to duplicate and eternalize the personality and its individuality in artistic production (*AA*). Dominated by the will and its desire for self-glorification and self-perpetuation, the artist "strives to be deathless through his work" (*AA*). In his "creative lordliness" the artist seeks to "become God" (*AA*).

The creative will of the artist on the one hand aspires to "a deliberate denial of all dependence" through a "creative impulse that seeks to bring forth the world and itself from itself and without help" (*AA*), but on the other hand, such "splendid isolation" is perpetually threatened by the artist's need for mirroring affirmation from others—for applause, recognition and fame (*AA*). Not surprisingly, Rank is especially mindful of the narcissistic components in the artist's "love" relationships. Thus, the artist requires not only public approbation, but also "an individual 'public,'" "a single person for whom ostensibly he creates," "a concrete Muse through whom or for whom the work is produced" (*AA*). Typically, the artist depends on his love objects to satisfy his "craving for a Muse" (*AA)*, who will function as a mirroring, echoing, approving and narcissistically sustaining presence. Hence, the artist's relation to his lover "has more of an ideological [narcissistic] than a sexual significance." (*AA*).

According to Rank, although the creative type is more successful than the neurotic in dealing with the "fundamental problem of the Self," the artist has in common with the neurotic the same "exaggerated fear of ... the destruction of the Self" (*BP*). As in the neurotic, the rock-bottom fear in the artist is the dread of self-dissolution and self-loss. The artist must withhold himself from "complete surrender" to experience "because he fears he will become completely absorbed in it" (*AA*). Seeking to "protect himself against the transient experience, which eats up his ego," the artist "takes refuge ... from the life of actuality, which for him spells mortality and decay," and "substitutes artistic production for life" (*AA*). Creative production, through the fantasy of self-immortalization in the work of art, thus serves to sustain self-integrity and ward off the spectre of self-disintegration.

In both *Art and Artist* and *Beyond Psychology* Rank makes frequent mention of a "fundamental dualism," or core conflict, which lies at the heart of the artistic personality. This core conflict appears in numerous interrelated guises: self-assertion *vs* self-negation, dominance *vs* surrender, separation *vs* unification, differentiation *vs* identification, difference *vs* likeness, dissimilation *vs* assimilation, affirmation of individuality *vs* immersion in the collectivity, the dread of life (individuation) *vs* the dread of death (reabsorption and de-differentiation), etc. Rank conceptualizes all such dualities within the artist as expressions of a pervasive and fundamental conflict between "the two essential forms of self-perpetuation" (*BP*). In one form the individual strives directly to preserve, aggrandize and eternalize his own individual self (e.g., in his creative products). In the other form he attempts to gain self-perpetuation vicariously, through passive surrender and participation in the immortality of some glorified higher power (such as a culture hero, God, or the community itself). These two forms of self-perpetuation bear a close resemblance to the two archaic pathways, described by Kohut (1971), along which an individual may seek to restore, sustain and regulate a threatened or crumbling self-representation: through the affirmation of the primitive grandiose self or through merger with an idealized, omnipotent object. Since Rank viewed the artist as being perpetually torn between these two modes of narcissistic reparation, and since Rank clearly identified himself with the artist, we should not be surprised to learn that Rank's own life was pervaded by a continuously oscillating struggle between his own powerful grandiose wishes on the one hand and his equally strong yearnings for union with an omnipotent object on the other. Nor should we be surprised to discover that the painful repetitive cycle of forming and severing attachments to supporting ideologies and idealized others, which Rank ascribed to the artistic type (*AA*), was actually "the picture of his own struggle with life" (Taft 1958).

To sum up: through an elucidation of the various "narcissism themes" which pervade his writings, we have attempted to demonstrate that Rank's theory of personality is essentially a theory of the narcissistic realm of personality; that his theory of neurosis is a theory of narcissistic disorder; and that his theory of therapy is a theory for the treatment of narcissistic disturbances. Indeed, the development of Rank's theories over the thirty-four year course of his writings may be viewed as a process of progressive synthesis, abstraction, generalization (and, at times, rationalization) of the narcissism themes into a comprehensive psychology of man. This process of theoretical consolidation reached its culmination in his concept of the will, which reified the subjective experience of grandiosity and elevated it to the position of the central metapsychological principle governing human conduct. There is no doubt that Rank's insights into the mysteries of narcissistic phenomena were acute. At the same time, his emphasis on narcissism to the nearly total neglect of more differentiated love/hate attachments eventuated in a narrowly one-sided view of human psychology. We shall now turn to Rank's own life in an effort to locate the roots of both his understanding of, and his one-sided attention to, narcissism.

RANK'S LIFE

The analysis of Rank's life which follows is by no means intended as a complete psychobiography. We shall attempt only to document the existence of a pervasive narcissistic disturbance in Rank's personality, and to elucidate some of the developmental origins and characterological consequences of this disturbance, including especially its profound impact on his theory-building. Other aspects of Rank's life and personality will not be covered. As our source of data we shall rely primarily on the biography of Rank composed by Jessie Taft (1958)[2], his longtime colleague, disciple, friend and Muse. In addition to Taft's own personal recollections of Rank, the biography contains excerpts from Rank's four diaries, or "Daybooks," which span about two and one-half years of his life, from age eighteen through twenty-one, along with numerous letters that Rank sent to Taft during their long correspondence.

First we shall consider some of the clinical manifestations of narcissistic disturbance in Rank's personality. Next, we shall explore some of the possible developmental origins of this disturbance. Then we shall attempt to reconstruct the reparative efforts with which he reacted to these developmental traumata. And finally, we shall take up the issue of the subjectivity of his theories.

Evidence of Narcissistic Disturbance

Clinical evidence of a narcissistic disturbance in Rank's personality can be found in the patterning of his mood swings, in his lifelong tendency of grandiose isolation, and in the quality of his object relations.

Mood disorder. That Rank suffered from a rather serious disturbance in self-esteem regulation can be easily inferred from the often cataclysmic mood swings which seem to have pervaded his entire adult life. Examples of his narcissistic vulnerability and the extreme fluctuations in his self-esteem, which were intimately connected with the relative paucity or abundance of his creative output, can be found in two entries in his "Daybook" as early as age nineteen:

What do I value in myself? .... Nothing! I shall live in vain. As I am not able to live a full life and also can create nothing whole, so my pride decides to pass away wholly and completely without value [pp. 7–8].

There are moments in which I believe firmly in my high endowment and therein that I belong to those who, even if they are not immortal, still live on for several centuries in their works. In such moments I have an indescribable feeling of happiness, although I know that it is empty. If I have erred, then will come a disillusionment so frightful that I shall never overcome it [p. 8].

Swings between experiences of narcissistic fullness and emptiness, inflation and depletion, hypomania and depression, are also recorded at twenty:

I fell into feverish activity, I worked from eight to ten hours a day, and collected an immense amount of material. Suddenly in one day, as if in ecstasy, I wrote down a four-act drama.... Then my genius broke through with elemental force. I became ... like a lightening conductor of God.... Upon these periods of restless tireless activity there followed a time of inactivity and exhaustion that seemed very serious and made me doubt my abilities .... A poet is like a sponge. He absorbs himself in an experience, an adventure.... There follows of necessity a time of thinness, dryness, and emptiness until a new life experience stirs him up again [p. 26].

The extreme oscillations in his mood and self-esteem remained with him into his middle years. At forty, he wrote a letter to the Freudian inner circle, in which he referred to his "manic-depressive swings, which...were usually related to the periods of extreme creativity with their aftermath of exhaustion." Between the ages of forty-nine and fifty-two a series of letters to Taft suggests that the inevitable narcissistic injuries and frustrations of middle age (e.g., dwindling physical and mental capacities, fading dreams, and approaching spectres of helplessness, dependency and death) had plunged him into severe depression. He writes of a total loss of interest in patients, writing, reading, success, fame—in everything. At fifty-two, he wrote to Taft despairingly:

I felt lately ... that I am dead! ... I feel dead ... [p.218].

And soon thereafter:

> The wild duck when wounded is supposed to go all the way
> down to the ground, bite into it, and stay there till it dies ....
> At present I am going to the ground... [pp. 222–223].

But at fifty-four, about seven months before his death, his self-
esteem soared again as he enjoyed a renewed burst of creative
activity:

> With me it was always that I was bigger than the work .... I am
> still bigger.... I always seem to rise one mile or so above the
> place on which I am actually operating or creating [p. 257].

He referred to himself as being in a state of "stratospheric
compensation." And then:

> I am still in the stratosphere and hope to remain there—
> because it seems the only place where I can breathe now
> [p. 258].

Rising to the stratosphere and biting into the ground and dying
like a fallen duck: clearly Rank was offering a self-description
when he described the neurotic as "wavering between his
Godlikeness and his nothingness" (*TR*).

That the disturbance in self-esteem regulation and extreme
mood swings may have covered a dangerous fragility in his self-
representation along with a looming threat of self-fragmentation is
suggested by three recorded occurrences indicative of severe
narcissistic decompensation. The first occurrence, described in an
"Autobiography" which was part of his first "Daybook," took
place when he was an adolescent. Rank's father, a heavy drinker
who complained often of head pains, came home in a "drunken
frenzy." The father "bellowed hoarsely and struck his hands
against the table till they bled," while the young Rank "sat
motionless in a corner as if turned to stone." He began to
experience "exhaustion" in his limbs and "severe head pains," and

became acutely hypochondriacal. Then he retreated into grandiose detachment:

> I became an ever more attentive observer of my illness.... I myself had been weak and no good from birth, and have perhaps no single bodily part that is completely right.... Shortly there remained for me no doubt: it was the first signs of the beginning of brain paralysis.... It grew hard for me in this instance ... just to maintain my sanity. And yet a few weeks later I drew from it an untroubled indifference so light that from then on, I derided all the little human needs [pp. 16–17].

He then immersed himself in the writings of Nietzsche:

> I left gladly my dark cold milestone and ... I bathed, as it were, in Nietzsche's spirit and got a charmed, weatherproof, bulletproof skin, that should protect me in the meantime against external attacks.... I had not to go forward but to fly upward [p. 17].

Clearly, the father's frightening drunken frenzy, representing both a shattering disappointment in the father and an equally shattering dramatization of young Rank's vulnerability and powerlessness in the face of the frenzied father, had inflicted a profound narcissistic wound. At the brink of narcissistic decompensation (symbolized by brain paralysis), Rank recoiled into a regressive preoccupation with a fragmented body-self (hypochondriasis). He then apparently warded off further decompensation by a reparative retreat to grandiose indifference and invincibility through identification with the omnipotent Nietzsche.

A second experience (or group of experiences) pointing to the extreme precariousness of his self-representation is described in an entry in his Daybook at nineteen:

> Many times I read my thoughts as though they were those of another: it doesn't occur to me at all that I could have written

it, and I would like to meet the man who has composed it. Is it that I am in another state when I write? Is it a higher one? I see in myself no steadily growing development but one by leaps and bounds [p. 21].

The entry alludes to depersonalization experiences and to a marked lack of cohesion and temporal stability in the self-representation: profound disturbances in the feeling of self-continuity and personal identity.

The third occurrence indicative of serious narcissistic decompensation is described in an entry made in the "Daybook" at twenty. Rank had been forced by the necessity of earning a living into the humiliating situation of having to take a menial job in a machine shop. The extremely mortifying quality of this experience, along with the "hollowness, emptiness, and aimlessness" of his existence during this period, had plunged him into deep despair, such that he was at the brink of suicide. Apparently he attempted to restore his crumbling self-representation through a massive immersion in grandiose fantasy and frantic mental activity:

Myriads of thoughts would go through my head so fast that they could keep pace with my breathing, so that I never once had time even to write them all down. I am of the opinion that in the last five years I have experienced and learned more than formerly the whole race during its existence; but the almost sick brain activity that took place with me on a few days of the last month exceeded all that had gone before. I felt as if the questions struck my brain as the thoughts from a small center made ever wider circles, in order finally to break on the borders of the unthinkable, just as a little stone that has been thrown into the water causes ever larger rings that finally dissolve on the shore without trace. My head hurt me terribly, I had fever, and was close to madness [pp. 27–28].

Again the threat of fragmentation and self-dissolution, this time as he felt himself to be flooded with reactive grandiosity and a hypomanic flight of ideas. Interestingly, Rank was able to reconstitute himself by writing a letter asking for rescue and support from an apparently imaginary idealized benefactor, a prophetic foreshadowing of his meeting with Freud about a year later. Further, we suspect, as did Taft, that on many occasions throughout his life Rank, like his genius type, reverted to his creative intellect and gift for conceptualization to bring "order, meaning, and control into the psychic chaos" (*AA*) which threatened him with self dissolution.

Splendid isolation. The phrase "splendid isolation" encompasses a triad of interrelated characterological tendencies which frequently occur together: grandiose self-inflation along with devaluation of others; isolation and withdrawal from overt interpersonal relationships along with an intense self-preoccupation; and a lack, paucity or shallowness of love/hate attachments to others. Evidence for all three tendencies can be found in Rank's personality.

Rank's autobiographical "Daybooks" as well as his major theoretical writings abound in examples of his grandiosity, largely transposed into the intellectual sphere. For instance, he opens his first "Daybook" at eighteen with a statement of his intellectual ambitions:

> I want to make progress in psychology. By that I understand
> ... the comprehensive knowledge of mankind ... which only a
> few souls have tried to reach [p. 4].

A bit later he offers an improved version of the Ten Commandments. At nineteen he sets down an outline of a staggering intellectual program which he hoped to complete in the near future: a novella, a novel, four dramas, eight poems, a discussion of the seasons, three essays (on religion, education, and the world), and the composition of his last will and testament. A passage that follows indicates that his grandiose expectations of intellectual perfection could sometimes become a painful burden:

> I would like to improve every sentence. Nothing is good

enough for me. This work disgusts me. What is not successful
for me at the first attempt, has already failed [p. 22].

Shortly before turning twenty-one Rank wrote, in an obvious self-
reference: "Every great thinker holds himself to be the apex of
evolution. That faith is the noblest kind of egoism" (p. 49).

At twenty-one Rank expresses his confidence in his illusory
omniscience, as well as his dismay at the dilemma it creates for him.

Now I see everything clearly: the world process is no longer a
riddle. I can explain the whole culture, yes, I can explain
everything. What shall I be able to do with the remainder of
my life? [p. 52].

And along with his grandiose self-inflation went a deep scorn
and contempt for others, for his "stupid, sensation-hungry
compatriots" and "less gifted, weaker men." At nineteen:

If anything could drive me to suicide, it would be the stupidity
and commonness of mankind.... The most stupid of my
acquaintances was the most use to me. With everything that I
wanted to comprehend, I always thought about it as if I had to
make it clear to him [p. 20].

At twenty:

Up to now I have known no living man whom I would have
considered more complete in every respect than myself....
The people with whom I became acquainted were usually so
confined, little, narrow, and suffering that I was glad to come
away from them.... In relation to their nullity, I learn to prize
my worth all the more [pp. 29–30].

One need only scan Rank's major theoretical writings to
recognize that intellectual grandiosity remained a permanent
feature of his personality throughout his adult life. Even Jessie
Taft, his at times worshipful disciple, noted Rank's "assertions of

omniscience." (Incidentally, we noticed in ourselves an at times considerable irritation brought on not only by Rank's extravagant intellectual claims, but also by his contempt for other thinkers, manifested in the ease with which he dismisses theories which are in opposition to his own.)

Rank's isolation and insulation from human contact was apparent throughout his life. Referring to his loneliness during adolescence, he wrote in the "Autobiography" in his first "Daybook" with obvious bitterness:

> About this time I found the lack of friends very painful. Now I find this loss no longer deep, for I have learned that friends are mostly a prop or a burden...[p. 14].

At nineteen he entered in a "Daybook" that "I feel for most people no sympathy, only for animals...." (p. 22), for in animals he could find a representation of his own frightened, sad, and vulnerable self. As to humans, however:

> I have an aversion to every contact with people, I mean even to every physical contact. It costs me an effort to extend my hand to anyone, and if I must do it, I first put on gloves. I couldn't kiss anyone.... I cannot bring myself to share my manuscripts with anyone [pp. 22–23].

His profound need to isolate himself from the rest of humanity is poignantly expressed in his plans for his eventual burial, written down at nineteen:

> I wish to lie alone outside all cemetery walls and boundaries [p. 23].

At twenty he wrote:

> I stand outside, an unrelated spectator [p. 43].

In Taft's account of Rank's later years we find that isolation from others and "deprivation of all but the most limited form of group understanding and support" was as much a part of his life then as it had been earlier. At one point Taft even voices a suspicion that his grandiose and self-insulating tendencies may have contributed to Rank's untimely death, by an infection at fifty-five:

> Always he feared drugs and insisted that his organism refused to accept them. An undoubtedly irrational sense of the inviolability of his body as well as his spirit may have worked against a cure [pp. 266–267].

Hand in hand with Rank's isolation and withdrawal went an intense absorption in his self and in his internal processes. When he was nearly twenty-one, he entered in his "Daybook:"

> Self-observation is not only one of the most wonderful but also one of the most rewarding capacities of man. Thus I know nothing more interesting than me myself, than my development [p. 45].
> I have been alone for the longest time. Entirely concentrated on myself. I associate only with me myself, with forms that I create [p. 48].

At times Rank's fascination with his own inner processes became a painful "burden" that "grows like an avalanche" which threatened to overwhelm him. And his self-preoccupation continued throughout his later years. A series of letters to Taft, at forty-nine, were filled with references to his "former self," "old self," "new self," "natural self," "whole self," etc. When frustrated by external circumstances and the narcissistic blows of middle age, he also wrote to her at fifty-two:

> I had enough of the "world" and I have worlds and worlds within myself [p. 223].

As Taft notes on several occasions, Rank rarely tired of observing, conceptualizing, and writing about his own self-development.

As one might suspect, along with the narcissistic trends in Rank's personality went a paucity and a certain shallowness of love/hate attachments to others. In a "Daybook" entry made at twenty Rank himself seemed to question the depth of his connectedness to and involvement in real aspects of the object world:

> In all things I recognize and wonder at the manifold connections that unite me with them.... It is, however, also possible that things have no affinity to me at all but that I... project upon the things, reflect into them, mirror myself in them... [p. 29].

Both the degree of his self-absorption and a shallowness in his object relatedness are suggested in an entry made just before he turned twenty-one:

> What I see [outside of his own self] is so horribly superficial that it is not worth the trouble of going to the bottom of it. The most exciting is introspection and the feeling of joy that streams through me in such moments [p. 45].

A similar shallowness of object relatedness, this time in relation to his patients, he communicated in a letter to Taft at forty-six:

> I am in need of them to make a living but I don't want them. I am just as glad if a patient does not turn up as if he does [p. 162].

Taft observed that Rank's therapeutic practice "became a burden that no longer held a challenge for him." A further piece of evidence for a certain shallowness in his object attachments is the abruptness with which he could abandon a friendship that was no longer consonant with his narcissistic needs. When Rank was forty-eight he even temporarily deserted the devoted Jessie Taft, out of a need to "rescue" his own self, "which was endangered."

Object relations. In line with these observations, one obtains in reading both the autobiographical and biographical material on Rank little sense of the real characteristics of the important figures in his life (parents, brother, wives, daughter); they simply do not emerge as flesh-and-blood persons. One cannot escape the impression that in large part Rank's object relations were in the service of his narcissistic needs; that is, they functioned primarily to restore, buttress, and maintain his precarious self-representation. In Rank's experiential world there seemed to be two distinct categories of objects, corresponding to two types of narcissistic transference. There were the idealized, omnipotent objects whose grandeur Rank sought to absorb through merger. And there were the "Muses" who sustained Rank's grandiose self-perceptions by serving as mirroring, echoing and approving presences.

During his youth Rank's yearnings for union with an omnipotent object found expression primarily in periods of nearly total immersion in studies of the works and lives of "illustrious men," periods of withdrawal from the "bogs of everyday" into the "Valhalla of great souls." His experience of merger and wish to absorb the object's greatness is captured in an entry written at nineteen:

> I seek to comprehend distinguished individuals always completely and at once. I strive to become acquainted with their collected works, but above all with their lives, their correspondence, and their diaries and first of all to comprehend completely the artist through the man. I then transfer myself so vividly into their thought world that I am not only inspired to create something similar in their form but often quite independently, before I know all their ideas, I pick up a theme that they have treated already [p. 7].

To that end he surrendered himself to the likes of Schopenhauer, Ibsen, Nietzsche, Wagner, Darwin, Napoleon, Jesus, and of course, Freud. An entry written toward the end of his twentieth year indicates that he occasionally envisaged seeking borrowed powers from his actual acquaintances as well, acquaintances who possessed abilities and strengths that Rank felt he lacked:

> Among the many people I know are three with whom I could perhaps associate for a long time.... What I lack, that I love in the three [pp. 46–47].

As to the Muses who reflected back images of Rank's grandiose self, foremost among them was Jessie Taft, who seemed always ready to provide empathic understanding, acceptance, approval, and admiration. His reliance for "narcissistic cement" on his relationship with Taft is conveyed in a letter he wrote to her at fifty-two:

> I realized that I never had a real sense of perpetuation or continuation and was glad you had it for me [pp. 226–227].

In another letter to Taft, written at fifty-four, he expressed his urgent need for Taft to experience and affirm his "new self" in order to lend it a sense of reality.

Anais Nin (1966), Rank's former analysand, claims in her diary that he also tried to persuade her to join him in New York to fill the role of Muse and disciple and thus revivify his existence. Indeed, to the extent that one can be convinced of the accuracy of her descriptions of her analysis with Rank, and particularly her accounts of Rank's long excursions during her treatment hours into his theoretical and philosophical ideas, one wonders about the degree to which Rank may have relied upon his patients as mirroring, echoing objects. Taft also alluded to the difficulty Rank may have had in meeting his "obligation to restrain his own creativity in favor of the patient."

Clearly, when Rank wrote in *Beyond Psychology* (1941) of the "tragic" circumstance that "the ego needs the Thou in order to become a Self," he was referring indirectly to his own need for narcissistic object relationship. Little material is presented in his biography of his relationships with his wives and daughter. One is left with the impression that his relationship with his first wife foundered in part because of her steadfast attachment to the Freudian movement which Rank had abandoned—i.e., her continued assertion of her separateness from Rank. His second wife was his former secretary, perhaps more amenable to the role of Muse. There are indications that he was devoted to his daughter. However, his theoretical emphasis in his writings on the parent's driving need to use his child as a vehicle for his own self-perpetuation is suggestive of a strongly narcissistic component in that relationship also. However, lest we have painted a too one-sided picture of the dominating influence of narcissistic strivings in Rank's object relations, we should note, for example, that both Taft and Nin (1966) have commented on Rank's gift for intuitive empathic understanding of others' internal processes. Taft reports also that during periods of his later life Rank was able to take "Sabbatical leave" from his narcissistic pursuits, to revive his more "natural, human self," and to turn more to real life, including especially his marriage.

Childhood Traumata

Having documented some of the clinical evidence for a narcissistic disturbance in Rank's personality, we shall now explore some of the childhood roots of this disturbance. In his brief "Autobiography," entered into his Daybook, at nineteen, Rank begins his account of his origins with suggestions of both his feeling of differentness and of massive narcissistic traumata:

> I was born ... with hair complete, as the third child of weak but apparently healthy parents. I followed the usual course from the first bath to teething ... only to fall back broken with the first milestone of my dangerous path. Joint rheumatism was there. One may not underestimate its influence on my life... [p. 10].

As to his parents during his early childhood:

> My father, who is a quiet drinker, wherewith it is not to be said that he is also quiet after the drinking, bothered himself little about me and my brother (my sister had died when a few months old) and my mother found her satisfaction in the fact that at least we lived, that is, had something to eat and went decently clothed. So I grew up, left to myself, without education, without friends, without books.... I did not even have a religion, to which I might have been able to appeal [p. 10].
> As I was also by nature somewhat rachitic, held by no one to a prudent way of living, and in my free hours was not watched over, I sickened early with joint rheumatism [p. 11].

According to Taft, Rank regarded his older brother with admiration and respect. However, during Rank's early childhood years his brother "had his own comrades, with whom he naturally associated more gladly than with me." Rank's frustrations continued on into the latency period, as his working-class parents failed to understand, appreciate, affirm and nurture both his emotional needs and unique gifts. His personality as well as his genius were early on forced to develop in a lonely emotional vacuum, devoid of narcissistic support.

Born of weak and neglectful parents; stricken from an early age with the debilitating conditions of joint rheumatism and rachitis; an alcoholic, sometimes violent father, totally indifferent and disinterested in his son; an unsophisticated mother who tended only to the boy's physical needs, unmindful of his needs for guidance and emotional sustenance: clearly, in his early years Rank suffered serious deprivations and shattering, repetitive narcissistic traumata in the areas of both the grandiose self and the idealized parent imago. Not surprisingly, in view of such massive narcissistic frustrations and disappointments, as a child he held "a deep rage inside," to which he dared not give vent because of his vulnerability and consequent fear of angry confrontation. Eventually he fled from his frustrations and rages into his daydreams and his books.

Also, not surprisingly, Rank as a young child began to show clinical signs of severe narcissistic disturbance. For instance, early on he developed an acute and preoccupying terror of death, a symptom of his narcissistic rage, of the vulnerability of his self-representation, and of the looming threat of narcissistic decompensation (see Stolorow 1974):

> Death ... became a problem to me above all.... I did not sleep for many nights and thought only about dying with terror and chattering teeth [p. 11].

Reparative Trends

How did the young Rank restore his severely damaged self-representation and ward off the danger of large-scale and irreversible narcissistic decompensation? As suggested in the earlier sections on Rank's grandiose isolation and his object relations, it appears that his efforts at narcissistic reparation followed both pathways mapped out by the two archaic configurations, the idealized parent imago and the grandiose self, at which his early narcissistic traumata had arrested his development.

His earliest attempts at narcissistic restoration probably took the form of regressive merger with an idealized mother imago. The seeds for such an idealization were undoubtedly planted by the mother's acknowledged ability to care for the infant's physical and elementary body-contact needs. The early restitutive merger experiences, consequent to narcissistic frustration, apparently laid the foundation for Rank's later intense identification with his mother, including his identification with the idealized prenatal and birth-giving mother. This latter identification is clearly seen in passages entered in his "Daybooks" when he was twenty, in which he compares his experiences of "carrying" an idea and developing a creative work with the mother's experience of the embryo quietly "ripening" within her.

Following his oedipal period, when Rank had achieved some sense of masculine identity, he turned (because of the total unavailability of his father and the partial unavailability of his brother) to certain "big men" outside the family in search of an idealized male figure with whom to identify. These efforts at narcissistic reparation through the omnipotent object met with disaster when one of these "gentlemen," during Rank's seventh year, provided him with "my introduction to erotic experience" which laid the "foundation stone of my later sufferings." This apparent sexual seduction apparently represented the crowning repetition of earlier traumatic disappointments by the idealized object. After that incident, and for the next fourteen years until his meeting with Freud, Rank largely abandoned his attempts to find an idealized figure in the real world. Instead he recoiled into derivatives of the grandiose self (withdrawal into splendid isolation, self-insulation and grandiose fantasy) as well as the pursuit of the omnipotent object (Schopenhauer, Nietzsche, etc.) on the safer terrain of the printed page. Even this latter terrain proved to be not without hazard, however, when at twenty he learned that Nietzsche had died of syphillis. Since Rank at this time relied heavily on his feeling of identification with Nietzsche, the disillusioning information again represented a grave narcissistic wound.

Clearly, as Taft points out, when Rank was introduced by Adler to Freud, and Freud was so impressed by Rank's early work on the artistic personality that he invited him into the psychoanalytic inner circle, Rank, at twenty-one, had at last found the yearned for union with the idealized parent imago that had been denied him throughout most of his earlier years. The early idyllic union with the omnipotent, omniscient Freud, and his involvement in the inner circle wrenched Rank out from his patterns of self-insulation and self-absorption. Taft observed that "the deepest relationship of his life was with Freud to whom, as his first ego-ideal, he yielded himself with a completeness never to be risked again" (p. 278). After about eighteen years, however, the long honeymoon of idealization became disturbed when Freud responded with reservations to Rank's book, *The Trauma of Birth*. In a letter to Freud, Rank angrily expressed his extreme disappointment and hurt that Freud had "misunderstood" his work. A further stinging disillusionment by the idealized Freud occurred upon the latter's confession that, although he had already criticized Rank's work, he had as yet read only half of it. Following these painful disappointments, Rank (and Freud) suffered several months of tormenting oscillation between Rank's urge to sever from Freud and his need to retain his strong attachment to Freud as an idealized object. It is an ironic example of the subjectivity of personality theory that it was *The Trauma of Birth* that seemed to signal the emergence of Rank's nascent ambivalent struggle to relinquish his narcissistic tie to Freud. Contrary to popular belief, the final break did not come about as a result of Freud ostracizing Rank. A careful reading of the Freud-Rank letters (excerpted in Taft 1958) during this difficult period indicates that the severance was primarily a result of Rank's profound disappointment and the attendant narcissistic rage in reaction to what he experienced as "flaws" in the idealized Freud. In a later, conciliatory letter Rank interpreted his urge to break with Freud as a direct reaction to the latter's serious illness and hence as an effort to "spare me the pain of a loss" (of the omnipotent object).

On another level, we think a shift was at this point taking place in the narcissistic transference-countertransference situation that had evolved between Freud and Rank. Rank was now clearly no longer satisfied to obtain borrowed greatness through surrender to the omnipotent object. With the writing and publication of *The Trauma of Birth*, noteworthy for its intellectual extravagances, Rank's own grandiose wishful self was rising more directly to the surface. Hence, he began to want from Freud not only omnipotence, but also an "understanding" (accepting, approving, mirroring) response to the manifestations of his own grandiose wishes. Freud, of course, was not about to function as anybody's echo; so he expressed the criticisms that he genuinely felt (asserted his separateness as an object), and hence frustrated Rank's wishes in the narcissistic mirror transference. The final outcome of this frustration and the rage it induced was Rank's angry break with Freud and recoil into his own at times grandiose theory-building in relative intellectual isolation. However, in the long, difficult period of ambivalent oscillation, during which Rank was torn between equally powerful drives to surrender and to break away, we see a dramatic manifestation of the fundamental dualism in Rank's personality that pervaded his life as well as his theories. We have attempted to show that this fundamental dualism represented a deep conflict in Rank between the two opposing modes of primitive narcissistic reparation: repair through merger with the omnipotent object, and repair through the affirmation of the grandiose self.

The Subjectivity of Rank's Theories

We have argued that every theory of personality is a system of ideas reflecting a domain of issues and dimensions of human experience and conduct which have become personally salient to the theorist as an individual (cf. Atwood and Tomkins 1976). This domain is structured by the formative experiences in the theorist's life, and particularly by those experiences which he has found to be most troubling and problematic. First, his theoretical view of essential or basic human needs will tend to mirror the needs which he has acutely felt himself. Second, his definition of the primary obstacle or dilemma in human life will reflect the issues which have most deeply challenged his own capacity to adapt to the world. And third, his vision of the ideal human state will represent a solution to his own most central problems and conflicts. In short, the structure of his metapsychology will duplicate the structure of his subjective representational world.

That these generalizations hold true for the subjectivity of Rank's theoretical system should already be abundantly clear from the theoretical and biographical material that has been presented. We have documented that certain "narcissism themes" with their associated narcissistic needs run through the evolution of Rank's theoretical position like red threads, and that the same narcissism themes and needs pervaded his own life experiences. In Rank's theorizing, the basic or essential human needs are narcissistic; and it was these narcissistic needs which he most acutely felt throughout his own life. In his theoretical writings, Rank posits a fundamental dualism between two opposing modes of narcissistic restoration: through merger with the idealized object, and through the affirmation of the grandiose self; and it was this fundamental conflict that was a central organizing feature in his own personal development. In his writings, Rank posits the primary obstacle or dilemma in human existence as the dread of self-dissolution, concretely symbolized in the dread of death; and clearly the ultimate danger against which he was compelled to protect himself in his own life was that of the disintegration and fragmentation of his self-representation, concretely symbolized in his lifelong struggle with death anxiety. Rank's theoretical vision of the ideal human state as the fully differentiated and individuated personality represents a solution to his own core problems and conflicts in the area of separation-individuation and self-object differentiation, rooted in the early traumata which arrested the development and articulation of his representational world. And finally, Rank's multifaceted conception of the will, which became the central metapsychological principle of his theoretical system, is perhaps best viewed as a highly condensed, reified symbol which crystallized his own personal history of successes and failures in his desperate quest for narcissistic reparation and a viable self-definition.

It is of particular interest that Rank himself was an early student of the subjectivity of personality theory. For instance, in *Psychology and the Soul* (1930), after noting some of the subjective sources of Freud's psychology, Rank states that he regards "psychology in general as an essentially projective affair, as an individual's attempt to create his own comfort and consolation" (p. 131). He further argues that "psychology is interpretation of self in others, just as physics is interpretation of self in nature. In this sense, psychology is self-affimation..." (p.195). *Beyond Psychollogy* contains similar glimpses into the subjective relativity of all psychological theories, including Rank's own. The intriguing question then emerges: What were the subjective origins of Rank's interest in and insight into the subjective origins of personality theory? We could reply that the pursuit of the subjective roots of personality theory is a further expression of Rank's stuggle with the difficulties he experienced in the area of self-object differentiation. Recall his comment (from a "Day-book") that "if the world is my projection, so is becoming conscious of this projection my birth" (Taft, p. 41). His efforts to tease the subjective from the objective in personality theory, to discriminate what is internal and external to the theorist, express Rank's own striving to differentiate his representations of the self and of the object world.

We cannot leave our study of Rank without commenting on the question of the contribution of narcissistic pathology to the productions of the creative genius (cf. Kohut 1971), which unmistakably Rank was. Clearly, what distinguishes Rank's achievement from that of less notable narcissistic personalities is that Rank's rich intellectual endowment was in some degree capable of successfully meeting the standards of his wishful grandiose self.

SUMMARY AND CONCLUSIONS

By documenting the various narcissism themes which pervade Rank's psychological writings, we have been able to demonstrate that in his theories of personality, neurosis, and therapy he essentially presents us with theories of the transformations, pathology, and treatment of narcissism. Indeed, his rich insights into the vicissitudes of narcissistic restoration are highly illuminating and of great clinical importance. Nonetheless, his one-sided focus on narcissistic phenomena to the exclusion of other sources of human conduct we found to be the product of his own subjective representational world and formative life experiences. Once again we have seen that through systematic psychobiographical analysis it is possible to highlight a theorist's unique contributions to understanding human personality as well as the limiting subjective influences which circumscribe the inclusiveness and general applicability of his metapsychological viewpoint.

NOTES

1. When references to Rank's works are cited within parentheses, they will be abbreviated as follows:

K	=	*Der Künstler.*
MBH	=	*The Myth of the Birth of the Hero.*
D	=	*The Double.*
TB	=	*The Trauma of Birth.*
WT	=	*Will Therapy.*
TR	=	*Truth and Reality.*
PS	=	*Psychology and the Soul.*
ME	=	*Modern Education.*
AA	=	*Art and Artist.*
BP	=	*Beyond Psychology.*

2. Unless otherwise indicated, all quotations in the section on Rank's life are taken from Taft's biography (1958).

REFERENCES

Atwood, G., and Tomkins, S. (1976). On the subjectivity of personality theory. *Journal of the History of the Behavioral Sciences* 12:166–177.

Goldberg, A. (1974). On the prognosis and treatment of narcissism. *Journal of the American Psychoanalytic Association* 22:243–254.

Jacobson, E. (1964). *The Self and the Object World.* New York: International Universities Press.

Kernberg, O. (1975). *Borderline Conditions and Pathological Narcissism.* New York: Jason Aronson.

Kohut, H. (1971). *The Analysis of the Self.* New York: International Universities Press.

Mahler, M., Pine, F., and Bergman, A. (1975). *The Psychological Birth of the Human Infant.* New York: Basic Books.

Nin, A. (1966). *The Diary of Anais Nin, Vol. 1: 1931–1934.* New York: The Shallow Press and Harcourt Brace and World.

Rank, O. (1907). *Der Künstler.*

——— (1909). *The Myth of the Birth of the Hero.* New York: Vintage Books, 1964.

———(1914). *The Double.* Chapel Hill: University of North Carolina Press, 1971.

——— (1924). *The Trauma of Birth.* New York: Harper and Row, 1973.

——— (1926, 1931). *Will Therapy* and *Truth and Reality.* New York: Alfred A. Knopf, 1972.

——— (1930). *Psychology and the Soul.* New York: A.S. Barnes, 1961.

——— (1932a). *Modern Education.* New York: Alfred A. Knopf.

——— (1932b). *Art and Artist.* New York: Alfred A. Knopf.

——— (1941). *Beyond Psychology.* New York: Dover, 1958.

Stolorow, R. (1970). Mythic consonance and dissonance in the vicissitudes of transference. *American Journal of Psychoanalysis* 30:178–179.

——— (1974). A note on death anxiety as a developmental achievement. *American Journal of Psychoanalysis* 34:351–353.

——— (1975a). Toward a functional definition of narcissism. *International Journal of Psycho-Analysis* 56:179–185.

—— (1975b). The narcissistic function of masochism (and sadism). *International Journal of Psycho-Analysis* 56:441–448.

Taft, J. (1958). *Otto Rank: A Biographical Study Based on Notebooks, Letters, Collected Writings, Therapeutic Achievements and Personal Associations.* New York: Julian Press.

CHAPTER 6

Psychoanalytic Phenomenology and the Psychology of the Representational World

In the preceding chapters we have demonstrated that metapsychological systems may be fruitfully analyzed from a psychobiographical perspective, as psychological products rooted in the formative life experiences of their creators. We have seen that a psychobiographical approach to a personality theory makes possible an unveiling of the concrete knowledge about persons embedded in (as well as obscured by) its metapsychological constructions. In the present chapter our purposes are threefold: First, we intend to draw out the implications of our psychobiographical researches for a critique of metapsychology, with special reference to the defensive function of theoretical reifications. Second, we shall offer some proposals for the creation of a metapsychology-free framework for the study of human personality. And third, we shall discuss some of the implications of adopting such a framework for psychodiagnosis, for psychoanalytic therapy, for the problem of "schools" of psychoanalytic thought, and for the conduct of personality research.

Of all the "schools" of personality theory, only classical psychoanalysis has seen its metapsychology subjected to thorough-going, systematic critiques on philosophical and scientific grounds, and we shall begin with a review of this critical literature. The material to be reviewed dovetails with and complements the conclusions drawn from our psychobiographical studies, and provides a backdrop against which their cogency and significance can be evaluated.

CRITIQUES OF PSYCHOANALYTIC METAPSYCHOLOGY

The problem of metapsychology, as distinct from clinical theory, has become the subject of lively theoretical controversy within classical (i.e., Freudian) psychoanalysis (see Gill and Holzman 1976). In Freudian theory the term *metapsychology* is generally used to refer to those propositions which attempt to "explain" clinical psychoanalytic observations in terms of hypothetical energies, forces, and structures which are presumed to actually and objectively "exist" (Gill 1976, Klein 1976). Among the numerous criticisms of Freudian metapsychology, we can distinguish those which object to particular metapsychological constructs, and those which question the entire metapsychological superstructure.

By the former, Freudian drive theory, with its energy-discharge model (the so-called "economic point of view"), has been especially singled out for criticism (Kubie 1947, Apfelbaum 1965, Holt 1965, 1967, 1976, Rubinstein 1967, Dahl 1968, Yankelovich and Barrett 1970, Peterfreund 1971, Arlow 1975, Basch 1976, Klein 1976). According to the drive theory, normal and pathological develop-ments of the personality are to be explained by the vicissitudes of the instinctual drives as they press to discharge their accumulating energies (Freud 1915). Holt (1976) states that Freud and his followers fallaciously used motivational concepts, such as instinctual drive and drive energy, as if they were real, concrete, causally efficacious entities. To Holt such thinking is a relic of nineteeth-century physics and physiology, the product of Freud's efforts to remain true to teachings by Helmholtz, Brücke and Meynert, which he absorbed during his medical and neurological training. Holt impressively supports his thesis that the theory of instinctual drives and energies "is so riddled with philosophical and factual errors and fallacies that nothing less than discarding the concept of drive or instinct will do" (p. 159). Rubinstein (1967) argues that the psychoanalytic conceptions of energy charge and discharge are inconsistent with current knowledge in neurophysiology and should therefore be eliminated.

From a somewhat different perspective, Klein (1976) demonstrates that the metapsychological conception of sexuality, in terms of an impersonal, quasi-physiological force that mechanistically presses for discharge, has actually obscured Freud's unique clinical contributions to the understanding of the personal meanings and of the particular motivational importance of sensuous experiences for the developing individual. Arlow (1975) argues that Freud's mixing of metapsychological propositions regarding psychic energies with his clinical formulations of intrapsychic conflict introduced confusion into psychoanalytic theory. Other writers have held the drive and energy concepts responsible for most of the conceptual difficulties that have accompanied attempts to understand the phenomena of narcissism and narcissistic disturbances (Pulver 1970, Stolorow 1975a) and for retarding the psychoanalytic investigation of schizophrenia (Holzman 1976).

Various other metapsychological constructs have also been subjected to criticism. To Holt (1975), for example, the id, ego and superego (the central constructs of Freud's "structural theory") often appear in metapsychological formulations as soul-like entities which are the products of reification and personification. For Peterfreund (1975) the use of such structural concepts to "explain" clinical observations results only in empty tautologies.

These objections to metapsychological constructs have been more or less circumscribed. We now come to those which question the validity and utility of the metapsychology as a whole. Among these we distinguish two groups: those which view Freudian metapsychology as inadequate and seek to replace it with a better one; and those which object to metapsychology *per se* and seek to eliminate it entirely from psychoanalytic theory.

Rubinstein, Peterfreund, and Kubie exemplify the first of these. Rubinstein (1967, 1976) would discard most of psychoanalytic metapsychology on the grounds that it is inconsistent with current knowledge in neurophysiology. He argues, however, that metapsychology—propositions which explain subjective experiences in terms of biological states of the organism, specifically, states of its brain—is necessary in order to justify and legitimize clinical hypotheses, particularly those concerning unconscious mental contents. He proposes, therefore, merely to replace current metapsychology with a new metatheory which is "protoneurophysiological"—that is, which points to neurophysiological events and is compatible with neurophysiological knowledge. Peterfreund (1971, 1975), in a similar vein, proposes to replace traditional metapsychology with more modern concepts derived from systems theory and information-processing models.

Kubie (1975) has been voicing his objections to metapsychology for at least thirty years. He comes close to a position we also hold:

> The realization is growing that quantitative analogies drawn from muscular effort, from hydraulic engineering or from the concepts about electricity which were current at the turn of the century do not provide appropriate models, appropriate metaphors or appropriate tools of communication, rumination or for testing the reality of psychoanalytic concepts. The muscular metaphors are especially misleading, because they depend on *projections outward from the inner subjective experience* of effort [p. 11; italics added].

For Kubie, furthermore, metapsychological theorizing—which casts the human psyche in the image of a biological machine understood in terms of levels, systems, structures, and quantities— always involves analogical, metaphorical thinking and reified projections of inner subjective experiences. Nonetheless, and despite his awareness of the pitfalls of such analogies and metaphors, he, like Rubinstein and Peterfreund, advocates merely the replacement of old-fashioned metapsychology with more sophisticated "machine models" drawn from modern mathematics and physics.

Those who object to metapsychology *per se* and seek to exorcize it altogether from the conceptual domain of psychoanalysis come closer yet to our own position. They are Schafer, Home, Gill and Klein.

In a series of provocative articles, Schafer (1972, 1973, 1975, 1976) has developed the argument that the structural-energic constructs of metapsychology represent unlabeled spatial metaphors, concretistic reifications of nonsubstantial subjective experiences (notably, vivid fantasy experiences). Metapsychological concepts such as psychic structure, force, and energy treat subjective states as though they were thing-like entities possessing such properties as substance, quantity, extension, momentum, and location. Schafer proposes a new "action language" for psychoanalysis. This would do away with mechanistic metapsychological reifications and would focus on the person-as-agent—that is, on the person as a performer of actions who (consciously and unconsciously) authors his own life. Within this "action language," the subject matter of psychoanalytic conceptualization and interpretation would become "action" itself (especially disclaimed action), as well as the individual's (conscious and unconscious) personal reasons for his actions (as opposed to their impersonal causes).

We are impressed with Schafer's approach. Our one reservation is to question whether an exclusive focus on the person-as-agent can deal with a patient's subjective experiences when the sense of "self-as-agent" (Schafer 1968) has remained undeveloped or has been atrophied.

Home (1966), Gill (1976) and Klein (1976) have largely clarified the distinction between psychoanalysis's metapsychology and clinical theory. Metapsychology and clinical theory, they hold, derive from two totally different universes of discourse. Metapsychology deals with the material substrate of subjective experience; it is couched in the natural science framework of impersonal structures, forces, and energies, while clinical theory deals with intentionality and the personal meaning of subjective experiences (for example, as disguised wish-fulfillments, self-punishments, or defensive maneuvers), seen from the perspective of the individual's unique life history. Clinical psychoanalysis asks "why" questions and seeks answers in terms of personal reasons, purposes, and individual meanings; metapsychology asks "how" questions and seeks answers in terms of the "nonexperiential realm" (Sandler and Joffe 1969) of impersonal mechanisms and causes. Home, Gill, and Klein maintain that the natural-science framework of metapsychology is completely inappropriate for the elucidation of the data of the psychoanalytic situation, but that clinical theory is uniquely applicable. They wish to disentangle metapsychological and clinical concepts, and to retain only the latter (now purified of mechanistic reifications) as the legitimate content of psychoanalytic theory.

Perhaps with the exception of Schafer, it is Klein (1976) who to date, has been the most prolific and systematic in his attempt to perform a radical "theorectomy" on psychoanalysis, cutting away the metapsychological overgrowth in order to unveil and clarify the "essential theoretical understructure," the "root principles" of clinical psychoanalysis. The essential psychoanalytic enterprise for Klein is the "reading of intentionality" or the "unlocking of meanings" from the text of a person's subjective experiences, and to this the concepts of the clinical theory are especially well suited, and metapsychology is totally irrelevant. Taking the experiencing person and his frame of reference as the point of departure, the clinical theory of psychoanalysis moves beyond "pure" phenomenology, says Klein, in that it includes assumptions about disavowed intentions and unconscious meanings—reasons, aims, purposes, and functions of which the individual is unaware. Furthermore, the clinical theory of psychoanalysis is concerned with the developmental origins of a person's experiential states, and focuses in particular on those experiential configurations (Klein uses the term *cognitive-emotional schemata*) which arise from the individual's efforts to resolve subjective emotional conflicts. For Klein the clinical constructs constitute a self-sufficient psychological theory (he spells it out in great detail) uniquely suited for guiding the investigation of data gleaned from the psychoanalytic situation. The "metapsychological contaminants" are not needed.

We would add that these critiques of Freudian metapsychology could apply with equal cogency, and with minor modifications only, to the metapsychological constructions of other personality theorists—for example, to the collective unconscious and its archetypes (Jung), to the Will (Rank), and to the orgone energies (Reich). Metapsychology—the inclination to explain subjective experiences by postulating impersonal entities, events, or processes assumed to exist objectively—is in our view a problem which has plagued not only classical psychoanalysis, but personality psychology in general. In short, we are in sympathy with Schafer, Home, Gill, and Klein.

METAPSYCHOLOGY AND THE REPRESENTATIONAL WORLD

Like other psychological products, metapsychology has multiple determinants and origins. One such determinant lies in the failure of personality psychology to fully differentiate itself from the imagery of the natural sciences, and the pervasive contamination of personality theories by metapsychological reifications is in part a symptom of this inadequate differentiation. As we noted in chapter 1, our four metapsychological systems bear the stamp of the particular scientific Weltanschauung prevalent in the cultural-historical setting in which they were created.

In our psychobiographical researches, where we sought additional origins of the metapsychological constructions, we demonstrated that the four metapsychological systems are in part reified expressions of their creators' most problematic subjective experiences. The metapsychologies, being experience-distant speculations remote from actual clinical observation, were ideally suited to serve as projective vehicles for aspects of their theorists' own representational worlds. The theorists' reifications, we have further shown, served specific defensive, restitutive, and reparative functions.

We have seen that aspects of Freud's theory of psychosexual development, which he "explained" (that is, justified) through reified conceptions of instinctual drives and instinctual energies, expressed Freud's wish to restore and preserve his idealized vision of his mother and to safeguard it from invasion by a profound unconscious ambivalence conflict. His metapsychological constructions were heirs to these defensive operations. Jung's metapsychological system embodied his lifelong struggle to defend the integrity and stability of his self against the danger of its obliteration through merger with omnipotent object imagos. The collective unconscious and its archetypes—the central reifications of his metatheory—crystallized his solution to the nuclear conflict of his existence, which was that between his need to preserve his precarious sense of self though withdrawal into a private world of self-sufficiency and omnipotent grandeur and his need to repair disrupted object ties and to recover a sense of union with others. Reich's metapsychological view of the personality in terms of the dialectics of the sexual life energies and the anti-sexual death forces we found to be the product of his subjective interpretation of his mother's suicide, for which he felt responsible. Through his eventually delusional reification of the omnipresent, all-enveloping orgone energies, which carried the imago of his reactively idealized mother, he undid the terrible trauma of her death and magically restored her to life. Rank's metapsychological reification of the Will encapsulated his efforts at narcissistic reparation, in which he organized his self-experience around grandiose images of personal omniscience and self-immortalization. His conception of the will-conflict as the fundamental motivational dynamic in human personality we found to reflect his oscillations between conflicting modes of narcissistic restoration.

From the juxtaposition of the subjective worlds of these four theorists as reflected in their metapsychologies emerged one further difference. The theoretical constructions of Freud and Reich stemmed from urgent attempts to protect and/or restore significant *object* imagos; those of Jung and Rank from an equally urgent need to sustain and/or repair a precarious *self*-representation. The predominance of self-imagery or object-imagery in an individual's defensive, restitutive, and reparative efforts, this finding suggests, may be a critical distinguishing characteristic of representational configurations in general.

In our four examples, metapsychological reifications performed functions analogous to those of character defenses. Through such reifications, each theorist's solutions to his own dilemmas and nuclear crises became frozen in a static intellectual system which, to him, was an indisputable vision of objective reality. His personal difficulties were justified, and his solutions to them strongly fortified against potential challenges, in that both were believed to reflect impersonal entities and events which universally determine the human condition. The closeness of these theoretical reifications to delusion construction becomes apparent. Indeed, in the case of Reich we witnessed the decompensation of more or less plausible metapsychologizing (plausible from the standpoint of the scientific Weltanschauung prevailing at the time) into overtly delusional ideation. We are tempted to propose (but we will not further investigate) the concept of reification as a ubiquitous defensive strategy appearing not only in systems of personality theory, but in a wide variety of psychological products, ranging from grand philosophical ideologies to highly idiosyncratic individual "personal myths" (Ehrenwald 1966) about the nature of the universe and human existence.

One or two clincial examples may serve to illuminate the parallel between reifications that function as pathological defenses and reifications in metapsychological theorizing. A young man, diagnosed borderline schizophrenic, was subject to terrifying states of extreme alienation, estrangement, and depersonalization, in which he pictured parts of his body as plastic, artifically constructed components of a mannequin. Periodically, he immersed himself in intense, reassuring, mystical experiences in which he believed that he "bathed in the central vibrations of the cosmos." These quasi-delusional, reified images of his connection to cosmic vibrations reflected his attempts to mend a disrupted sense of union with the object world and to restore the integrity of his dissolving self-representation. The reifications employed by this patient are, in their content and function, strikingly homologous to the Jungian vision of transcendent wholeness achieved through dialogue with the cosmic, archetypal forces of the collective unconscious.

A second young man, who sought treatment in order to restore some emotional spontaneity to his rigidly regimented life, believed that he possessed a limited supply of energy and bodily fluids which had to be conserved at all costs. He explained to his therapist that he could permit himself to have sexual relations only during the weekends, for fear that sexual activity on weekdays would so drain him of his energies and fluids that he would have insufficient amounts of these substances left over for the performance of his work. This imagery, which reified his dread of self-depletion (a nonsubstantial subjective experience) in terms of concrete substances, served the defensive function of providing him with an illusion of control—he imagined that he could conserve his energies and fluids (ward off self-depletion) by regimenting his sexual behavior. That this patient's defensive reifications are homologous to the classical Freudian notion of finite quantities of libido-substance which are discharged or bound within the mental apparatus is quite apparent. When such reified images are elevated to the status of theoretical postulates they more often than not lead to clinically indefensible suppositions (see Stolorow 1975a). One of us, for example, can recall a psychoanalytic instructor who woefully predicted the deterioration of Western technology on the highly questionable basis that, owing to the contemporary climate of sexual freedom and indulgence, young scholars would have little remaining libidinal energy available for intellectual sublimations!

TOWARD A PSYCHOANALYTIC PHENOMENOLOGY

Metapsychologies, we have attempted to show, are symptoms of the failure of personality psychology to differentiate itself from the natural sciences as an autonomous discipline and are also products of defensive reifications of the theorists' most problematic subjective experiences. The conclusions drawn from our studies have led us to an imposing problem: to develop a metapsychology-free framework for the study of human personality. Although their orientations differ somewhat from ours, Schafer (1972, 1973, 1975, 1976) and Klein (1976) have made significant strides in the same direction. Our approach, which we have tentatively christened "psychoanalytic phenomenology," takes the subjective "representational world" (Sandler and Rosenblatt 1962) of the individual as its central focus. We assume no impersonal psychical agencies or motivational prime movers in order to "explain" the representational world. Instead, we assume that this world evolves organically from the person's encounter with the critical formative experiences which comprise his unique life history.

Our four case studies may serve as examples of the application of this framework. For a psychoanalytic phenomenology, as exemplified in these studies, the units of analysis are the distinctive configurations of self- and object-representations which pervade subjective experiences. These configurations are distinguished not only by their ideational content, but also by their predominant affective coloring. Klein (1976) uses the term *cognitive-emotional schemata* to refer to such representational configurations; our only objection to this term is its somewhat experience-distant quality.

Once an individual has established a relatively stable representational configuration or, more broadly, a representational world, he will assimilate his subsequent experiences into its structure. Hence, his representational world will be discernible in the recurrent themes and leitmotifs which dominate his existence. As an example of this principle, our personality theorists imported their representational worlds directly into the thematic structure of their metapsychologies. Stable, recurrent representational configurations constitute the experiential referents for such terms as *character* and *personality structure*.

"Psychoanalytic phenomenology"—as distinct from metapsychology—does not postulate a theory of the nature of personality as an objective entity. It consists instead of a methodological system of interpretive principles whose aim is to guide the study of human experience and conduct. Furthermore, such interpretive principles need not assume that particular patterns of self- and object-representations (such as those embedded in the various metapsychologies) are central in the experiential worlds of all persons. Psychoanalytic phenomenology attempts to elucidate the *developmental origins* and *functional significance* (Klein 1976) of the representational configurations which pattern a person's subjective world. "Pure" phenomenology, in contrast, aims only at a detailed description of the modes of immediate experience. With regard to functional significance, clinical psychoanalytic observation has isolated at least five crucial functions that may be served by the representational configurations established during the course of a person's life history.

1. *Wish-fulfilling function.* A representational configuration may give expression to the person's most cherished wishes and urgent desires, to his goals and aspirations, and to the ideal states toward which he (consciously or unconsciously) strives. Clear examples of this function can be found in the classical psychoanalytic researches which unveiled the disguised wish-fulfillments represented in dreams, parapraxes, and neurotic symptoms. The wish-fulfilling function of representational configurations may be viewed along a developmental line spanning the diffuse, inchoate urges of the pre-verbal infant to the more or less articulated desires of the adult. Such wishes—in classical Freudian metapsychology—are derivatives of the sexual and aggressive instincts, reified in the concept of the id. In psychoanalytic phenomenology, however, the question of the "ultimate" (physico-chemical, biological) cause of any of these wishes is a natural-science issue tangential to the aim of understanding the meaning of a person's experience and conduct (Klein 1976).

2. *Self-guiding and self-punishing function.* A representational configuration may provide guidelines for morally acceptable behavior or for the maintenance of self-esteem, or it may give vent to the person's (conscious or unconscious) outrage at himself, or to the need to punish himself for trends which he regards as morally repugnant. An example of the latter would be a masochistic pattern of experienced victimization which stems from guilt and from a need to be punished for forbidden desires. In Freudian metapsychology, this function was reified in the concepts of the superego and ego ideal.

3. *Adaptive function.* A representational configuration may reflect the person's active (conscious or unconscious) efforts to cope with his sometimes overwhelming difficulties and crises. An example would be a configuration in which he actively repeats a passively experienced trauma with an eye toward mastering it. In Freudian metapsychology, this (and the following) functions were reified in the concept of the ego.

4. *Restitutive-reparative function.* A representational configuration may (consciously or unconsciously) restore or repair aspects of the self or of the object world which, in reality or in fantasy, have been lost or damaged. Jung's attempts to mend his ruptured object

ties by elaborating the concept of universally shared, transpersonal psychic contents would be an example. Another would be Reich's delusional resurrection of his dead mother in the form of the all-embracing orgone energies. Still another would be Rank's efforts to repair his traumatically depleted and chronically precarious self-representation through grandiose images of personal omniscience and self-immortalization.

5. *Defensive function.* A representational configuration may (unconsciously) serve to prevent the person from becoming aware of another configuration colored with intensely negative affect or associated with some anticipated extreme danger. An example would be the manner in which Freud's consciously idealized picture of his bond with his mother kept from his awareness his bitter disappointment in, and hatred of, her, which he associated with the danger of losing her. The elucidation of the defensive function of representational configurations in the context of a person's attempts to resolve subjective emotional conflicts is one of the most important contributions of Freudian clinical theory to psychoanalytic phenomenology (Klein 1976).

While conceptually distinguishable, these five functions are generally found to co-occur clinically, combined and amalgamated in highly complex ways. Any significant representational configuration will have multiple origins and serve multiple functions (Waelder 1936). The task of the clinician is to ascertain the relative motivational priority or urgency of each of these five functions by evaluating the meaning of a particular configuration for a particular patient at a particular point. Such an assessment of motivational or functional priority will directly determine the appropriate clinical intervention (Stolorow 1975b, Stolorow and Lachmann 1978).

We stress that these five functions do not require impersonal psychical agencies or motivational prime movers (e.g., the id, ego, and superego of classical psychoanalysis) to explain them. They represent, rather, a clinically useful classification of the conscious and unconscious purposes (Klein 1976) which the various representational configurations, established during the course of a person's life, may serve. Furthermore, this list of purposes or functions is not to be regarded as definitive or exhaustive. We envision, on the contrary, that heretofore undiscovered functions served by representational configurations will be illuminated through the continued application of the method of systematic, intensive case analysis. In our view the progressive enrichment of knowledge of such functions has constituted, and will continue to constitute, the essence of progress in the clinical psychoanalytic understanding of human personality.

The aim of psychoanalytic phenomenology is to elucidate not only the functional significance, but also the developmental origins of subjective representational configurations . This is an imposing task indeed, for it involves the formulation of a developmental psychology of the representational world which requires a comprehensive knowledge of both emotional and cognitive development. One of Freud's seminal contributions was his discovery of the manner in which early bodily sensations, sensuous experiences, and frustration-aggression sequences influence the development of the representational world. These contributions to clinical theory were obscured, as Klein (1976) has pointed out, through their contamination by Freud's metapsychology. We might add that a wide variety of early intense affective experiences, in addition to those involving sensuality and hostility, can leave their mark on the emotional coloration of the representational world (see Tomkins 1962, 1963).

Numerous authors have made important contributions to the elucidation of the normal and pathological vicissitudes of self- and object-representations as they evolve throughout the various developmental epochs (e.g., Fairbairn 1952, Jacobson 1964, Guntrip 1969, Kohut 1971, Mahler, Pine and Bergman 1975, Kernberg 1975). These contributions were often obscured through the continued introduction of metapsychological reifications in the form of psychical structures and agencies, instinctual drives and drive energies. Much of what we have to say about the development of the representational world is not new, based as it is on well-established clinical observations and formulations, such as those provided by the authors we have just listed. What is new is our suggestion that a clinically meaningful developmental psychology of the representational world, completely purified of metapsychological reifications, is possible.

Such a comprehensive developmental psychology would include a consideration of (1) the central issues which face the developing person, and the impact of his successes and failures to negotiate critical developmental tasks on the establishment of representational configurations; and of (2) the impact on the evolution of his representational world of his wish-fulfilling, self-guiding and self-punitive, adaptive, restitutive-reparative and defensive efforts during the various stages of the life cycle. In passing we note that a focus on the development of the representational world encourages the incorporation of the findings of nonpsychoanalytic investigators of perceptual and cognitive development, for example, Piaget (see Burgner and Edgcumbe 1972, Sandler 1975). Such syntheses have been rare in the history of personality psychology, largely because of incompatibilities among the metapsychological assumptions held by the various investigators.

We will not attempt to present a comprehensive developmental psychology of the representational world. We will limit ourselves instead to a consideration of two important developmental tasks—representational differentiation and integration—which have received a good deal of attention in recent clinical literature, and to an exploration of the impact of some common defensive operations upon representational configurations.

Representational differentiation and integration

In the earliest phase of infancy, self- and object-representations are undifferentiated. The neonate cannot discriminate between his own sensations and the objects from which they derive (Piaget 1937, Jacobson 1964). Hence, perhaps the first developmental task for an infant, central to the articulation and consolidation of his representational world, is the differentiation or subjective separation of self-representations from representations of his primary object, usually the mother (Mahler, Pine and Bergman 1975). An early infantile experience of partial self-object differentiation and partial self-object confusion would be the toddler who believes his mother knows his thoughts, or that she has put thoughts into his head—the normal developmental equivalent of the psychotic "influencing machine" (Tausk 1919).

A second characteristic of the infant's experience is his inability to integrate or synthesize representations with contrasting affective colorations. Thus, a second developmental task, coincident with that of self-object differentiation, is the synthesis of object representations colored with positive affects (for example, images of an "all-good" mother) and object representations colored with negative affects (for example, images of an "all-bad" mother) into an integrated representation of a total object with both positive and negative qualities, coupled with a similar synthesis of affectively contrasting self-representations into an integrated representation of the total self (Sullivan 1953, Kernberg 1975).

In object representations, the attainment of representational differentiation and integration is reflected in the achievement of "object constancy"—the capacity to sustain a differentiated and enduring image of another person valued for his real (positive and negative) qualities, and appreciated as an individual with his own needs and feelings (Burgner and Edgcumbe 1972). In the self-representation, differentiation and integration are reflected in the consolidation of a cohesive image of the self which is temporally stable and has an affective coloration more or less independent of immediate environmental supports (Stolorow 1975a). Such "self-constancy" has been described in terms of the subjective sense of identity (Erikson 1956), and in terms of the continuity of self-esteem (Jacobson 1964).

Failures to attain adequate differentiation and integration have been attributed largely to gross deficiencies in early maternal care as a consequence of severe psychopathology in the mother. Such deficiencies would include the mother's inability to respond empathically to her child's developmental needs; her extreme inconsistencies in behavior toward the child; and frequent exposure of the child to affectively unbearable sexual and aggressive scenes. The failure to attain adequate self-object differentiation, seen most dramatically in delusional merging of self- and object-images, has been implicated in predispositions to schizophrenic psychosis (Searles 1959, Kohut 1971, Kernberg 1975). However, varying degrees of difficulty in the area of self-object differentiation, as we see in the cases of Jung and Rank, can also be found in severe but non-psychotic personality disturbances. A narcissistic personality may require immersion in specific forms of object relationship in order to sustain his insufficiently consolidated self-representation (Kohut 1971). The failure to achieve adequate integration of representations with contrasting affective coloration, reflected most dramatically in rapidly alternating experiences of all-good and all-bad self- and object-images, has been implicated in the psychogenesis of the so-called borderline personality organization (Kernberg 1975, Atkin 1975).

It is possible to summarize the normal and pathological consequences of successes and failures in the tasks of differentiation and integration, we wish to emphasize, without recourse to metapsychological reifications of psychic structures, cathectic shifts, or fusions and defusions of drive-energies. This metapsychology-free conceptualization of early representational development, as we will show below, has important implications for psychodiagnosis, psychoanalytic therapy, and personality research.

Like the developmental tasks of differentiation and integration, common defensive operations can be conceptualized strictly and exclusively in terms of their impact upon a subjective representational world. To these we turn next.

Some Common Defenses

Repression and denial: Although the concepts of repression and denial are central to psychoanalytic clinical theory, analysts have had difficulty in defining them precisely, and in conceptually distinguishing them one from another (Stolorow and Lachmann 1975). Jacobson (1957), for example, emphasized that denial deals with perceptions of objective reality and repression with instinctual drive derivatives. A difficulty remained, however, in that in Jacobson's view perception is subject to denial, especially when instinctual conflict is associated with that perception.

The difficulties in attempting to discriminate between repression and denial—as well as the necessity for distinguishing between

them—derive from the contamination of these clinical formulations with metapsychological conceptions of instinctual drives and
drive energies. Repression and denial both involve the elimination
of something from awareness. The attempted distinction between
the elimination of drive derivatives (repression) and of perceptions
of reality (denial) is an artifact of metapsychology.

From the standpoint of psychoanalytic phenomenology, what is
eliminated from awareness through repression and denial is an
aspect of the representational world—specifically, a self-
representation, object representation, or self-object configuration
that is colored with intensely negative affect or associated with
some anticipated extreme danger. Clinically, "repression" is
usually restricted to the elimination from awareness of conflictual
representations of the self-as-subject or the self-as-agent (Schafer
1968); in typical clinical usage, that is, "repression" is directed
against representations of the self in which the person is actively
wishing for satisfactions, desiring objects, or striving for goals felt
to be morally abhorrent or highly dangerous. "Denial" is typically
used to refer to the elimination of conflictual representations of
objects and/or of the self-as-object (that is, of the self as an entity
existing in objective reality, an object of reality perception). Thus,
while a child "represses" his wishes (that is, eliminates from
awareness representations of himself as wishing), he "denies" the
reality of his parents' overwhelming power and of his own
limitations and helplessness (eliminates from his awareness these
aspects of his parents and of himself as objects existing in reality).
As used in the clinical literature, the term *denial* often also includes
the fantasies which the person substitutes for the denied reality
(that is, the wishful self- and object-representations which
he substitutes for those which are eliminated from awareness,
A. Freud 1937).

If we delete from our clinical formulations the metapsychological distinction between drive derivatives and perceptions of reality,
and if we recognize that both repression and denial operate upon
aspects of the subjective representational world, then, in our view,
the discrimination between repression and denial becomes
inconsequential. We would substitute for these two concepts the

notion of a primary defensive operation through which a person eliminates certain elements of his representational world from awareness. Then it becomes the *clinical* task to discern precisely what elements (object representations, representations of the self-as-agent or of self-as-object) are eliminated.

Other common defenses can be equally viewed (and clarified) as eliminating, or sustaining the elimination of certain elements of the representational world. For example:

Displacement: a representational configuration carries the affective coloring of a more dangerous one which has been eliminated from awareness;

Isolation: a representational configuration enters awareness stripped of its original dangerous affective coloration;

Reaction formation: the elimination of a conflictual self-representation (typically, a representation of the self-as-agent) is supported through the active cultivation of a contrasting self-representation;

Projection: dangerous contents of the self-representation are relocated in one or more object representations;

Incorporation: contents of an object representation are relocated in the self-representation;

Splitting: the segregation of representational configurations with opposing affective colorations.

These defenses are, in our view, transformations of subjective experience which eliminate from awareness aspects of the representational world that are colored with intensely negative affect, or are associated with some anticipated extreme danger. Particular defensive strategies may be especially suitable for specific experiential dilemmas. For example, incorporation is often called upon to ward off conflicts evoked by object loss (Freud 1917) and splitting seems designed to prevent experiences of intolerable ambivalence (Kernberg 1975).

These metapsychology-free formulations of the defenses are recommended for the conceptual clarifications which they achieve and for their implications for the precise framing of analytic interpretations.

IMPLICATIONS

Having offered some proposals for the creation of a metapsychology-free framework for the study of human personality, we have argued that the following three components constitute the necessary and sufficient ingredients for a clinically meaningful psychology of the representational world: (1) the distinctive configurations of self- and object-representations (including their affective coloring) which pervade a person's subjective experiences; (2) the developmental tasks (for example, representational differentiation and integration) which a developing person must negotiate in order to articulate and consolidate his representational world; and (3) the various functions (for example, wish-fulfilling, self-guiding and self-punishing, adaptive, restitutive-reparative, and defensive functions) that representational configurations may serve as they are established in the course of a life. Now we shall discuss some important implications of adopting such a framework.

Psychodiagnosis

We have noted that a number of authors have made statements about the connection between the state of a person's representational world and his psychiatric diagnosis. The failure to achieve adequate self-object differentiation, for example, has been viewed as inherent to the development of schizophrenic psychosis; inadequate representational integration has been linked to the development of the borderline personality. In such statements, analytically sophisticated clinicians graft correct and useful observations about a patient's representational world onto the existent psychiatric nosology, a system that has long been criticized for its attention to symptomatic manifestations to the neglect of psychogenesis. A more meaningful psychiatric classification system can be *derived from* considerations of the representational world than from the manifest symptom picture. Categorizing patients according to their degree of representational differentiation and/or integration rather than by their psychiatric symptoms is more meaningful clinically, in that such classifications have direct implications for the framing of therapeutic interventions. Ideally, we would "diagnose" a person by locating him in a multidimensional space according to the salient properties of, and dominant functions served by, the representational configurations which pervade his subjective experiences. Within our framework, in short, the primary task of psychodiagnosis becomes the detailed and systematic assessment of a patient's representational world.

Psychoanalytic Therapy

Our framework has direct implications for the conduct of psychoanalytic therapy. We contend that the therapist's evaluation of his patient's representational world strictly dictates the content of his interpretations and of his other interventions. A "good" interpretation has nothing whatsoever to do with metapsychological entities. An interpretation conveys the therapist's understanding of the nature, origins, and functions of the representational configuration currently structuring the patient's experiential world. In a defense interpretation, for example, the therapist will show his patient that the currently conscious configuration serves to prevent him from becoming aware of some other more negative or dangerous configuration. Interpretations are framed in the particular dialect of the patient's own subjective representational world, and not in the language of metapsychology.

As one of many possible examples of the importance of systematically evaluating the patient's representational world for the formulation of clinical interventions, we may cite the work of Stolorow and Lachmann (1978) on the distinction between defenses and their developmental pre-stages. They suggest that there is a developmental line for each defensive operation, and that a defense in the usual sense of the term represents the endpoint of a series of developmental achievements. Hence, it becomes clinically crucial to distinguish between a representational configuration that functions as a defense, and an apparently similar configuration that might be more accurately described as a remnant of an arrest at a pre-stage of defensive development.

Suppose, for instance, that a patient is experiencing a state of self-object confusion. The therapist must make a diagnostic determination as to whether this self-object confusion reflects the patient's use of defensive projection and/or incorporation, or whether it reflects an arrest in the development of his representational world at an early pre-stage of these defenses characterized by an inability to adequately differentiate self- and object-representations.

Or suppose a patient is experiencing rapidly alternating all-good and all-bad self- and object-images. Here the therapist must make a careful diagnostic judgment as to whether these unintegrated representations reflect the patient's use of defensive splitting, or an arrest in the development of his representational world at a pre-stage of this defense characterized by an inability to synthesize representations with contrasting affective colorations.

They stress that these diagnostic judgments directly guide clinical interventions. In the case of an arrest at a pre-stage of defense, the therapist will convey his empathic understanding of the experiential difficulties created by this developmental failure and will emphasize the patient's need to achieve adequate representational differentiation or integration. In contrast when a patient is using projection, incorporation, or splitting for defensive purposes, the therapist will offer interpretations of the dreaded representational configuration which the patient is thereby excluding from his awareness.

Schools of Psychoanalytic Thought

One of the more unfortunate developments in the psychoanalytic movement has been its division into separate "schools." The segregation and isolation of these schools from one another have deprived psychoanalysis of the enrichment that might ensue from their interaction and interpenetration. This division is along metapsychological lines and is largely on the basis of the unconscious resonance between the subjective concerns of the believers and the metapsychological dogma to which they adhere (Whitehead 1975). It follows that the creation of a metapsychology-free framework will foster the growth of psychoanalytic knowledge by making possible the inclusion of the contributions of theorists of varied metapsychological persuasions. All of the major schools of psychoanalytic thought have something to teach about the representational world.

For instance, with regard to our four major theoretical systems, Freud's formulations (and to some degree, Reich's) provide us with a profound understanding of representational configurations resulting from the clash of cherished wishes and urgent desires with moral prohibitions or anticipations of danger. Jung's work, when stripped of metapsychological reifications, offers a fascinating descriptive psychology of the vicissitudes of primitive self- and object-representations and their typical symbolizations. Rank's theories richly elucidate the quest for narcissistic reparation—the intricate pathways a person may follow in his efforts to shore up a damaged and precarious self-representation.

Other theorists contribute as well. Adler's work (Ansbacher and Ansbacher 1956) is a source of important insights into the role of the body-image in the development of the self-representation—in particular, the significance of a devalued body-image in the genesis of compensatory strivings for perfection and superiority. Horney (1950) contributes rich and detailed formulations regarding the developmental origins and functions of self-idealization and the search for glory. Fromm's (1941) early contributions enhance our understanding of the vicissitudes of separation and individuation, including the deep emotional resistances to this process which may persist throughout a life. And as a last example, Sullivan (1953) elucidates the role of anxiety in the early mother-child relationship in promoting and distorting the differentiation and integration of self- and object-representations.

We are clearly not advocating an uncritical and haphazard eclecticism which would apply metapsychological constructs from different systems as they seem to "fit." We are, on the contrary, suggesting a conceptual framework which takes the representational world as its central focus and eschews metapsychological reifications entirely. Such a framework opens the door to a synthesis of the contributions of the various psychoanalytic schools into a more general and inclusive theory.

Personality Research

A consistent focus on the subjective representational world of the individual has methodological and conceptual implications which reach beyond the construction of psychoanalytic phenomenology. In this section we shall discuss some of these implications for personality research and for a reorientation of personality psychology in general.

Carlson's (1971) lament, "Where Is the Person in Personality Research?" echoes the discontent of many personologists with the prevailing trends of academic personality research. Research designs which extract isolated "variables" in piecemeal fashion from the total phenomenological and life-historical context of personality contribute little to our understanding of persons. A conceptual framework which brings into focus the representational world of the individual holds great promise for reintroducing the intensive, in-depth case study as a principal methodology for investigating personality phenomena. In our four studies, we have sought to show that the distinctive configurations of self- and object-representations which pervade a person's subjective experiences constitute meaningful units of analysis for such a framework, and that it is possible to systematically elucidate the developmental origins and functional significance of these configurations. This is not to say that intensive case analysis should be the sole avenue for studying human beings, but rather that such analysis can be a continuing source of guiding theoretical ideas, and a means whereby personality psychology can recover its lost commitment to understanding the experience and conduct of persons.

As we argued in the opening chapter, one of the consequences of objectivist ideology is to subordinate theory construction to the narrower procedures of verification and proof. Psychologists persuaded by this orientation tend to regard frameworks already elaborated (such as the four we have studied) as biasing, distorting systems of unverified preconceptions. Hence, they argue for deferring new synthetic interpretations until investigators have established more accurately what "objectively exists" in the personality domain. We are not entirely unsympathetic with this line of reasoning, for many of the metapsychological suppositions of personality theories are not only unverified, they are intrinsically unverifiable, and they often obscure the theorists' unique contributions. But to envision the possibility of discovering anything important about man in the complete absence of guiding assumptions is to become entangled in the Husserlian fallacy. It is literally impossible to approach the phenomena of the world from a presuppositionless perspective. Every significant discovery is at the same time a constructive act of theoretical interpretation. The problem for personality research is therefore not how to divest itself of preconceived ideas and look upon man with pure and innocent eyes, but rather how to reformulate assumptions so as to guarantee more productive and conceptually unified lines of investigation. In our view, the premises embedded in the concept of the representational world are uniquely suited to this reorientation of the field, and these premises are capable of becoming a fruitful source of empirical and theoretical developments.

A Procedure for Exploring the Representational World

Structures of self- and object-representations can be studied in a variety of ways, including objective and even quantitative procedures. One such procedure is found in the recent innovative work of Rosenberg (1976). Rosenberg's research developed out of an interest in the problem of "person perception" in social psychology, and more particularly out of an interest in what social psychologists have called "implicit personality theory." This term refers to an individual's views about personality, to the traits he perceives as characteristic of himself and of others, and to his beliefs about the interrelations among these traits. It is described as "implicit" because it is inferred from the person's descriptions and expectations, rather than gathered from explicit statements by him. Most individuals could not in fact explicitly formulate their beliefs about others and themselves. "Implicit personality theory" can be seen as a subset of what, in the first chapter, we described as the implicit, prereflective background structures of the representational world.

Two problems have traditionally plagued studies of this topic. One of these pertains to a tendency among social psychologists to treat implicit conceptions and beliefs as self-contained empirical phenomena, isolated from the complex cognitive, emotional, and developmental context in which they crystallize.The second derives from an almost exclusive reliance on fixed-format instruments, such as trait checklists and rating scales. The particular trait categories are typically selected on an *a priori* and often fortuitous basis, and are then used as a framework within which all are constrained to respond. The accuracy with which the resulting trait attributions reflect the subject's idiosyncratic implicit conceptions becomes thereby highly questionable.

Rosenberg's solution has been to devise analyses which are sensitive to the unique sets of terms and organizing dimensions inherent in the subject's unconstrained, free descriptions of himself and others. Rosenberg has thus become increasingly involved with exploring the implicit personality theories of single individuals in the particular dialects of their subjective worlds. An early and especially interesting study (Rosenberg and Jones 1972) showed that a person's implicit view of people can be extracted from naturalistic material, such as a set of literary productions. The study concerned the novels of Theodore Dreiser. By applying the methods of clustering and multidimensional scaling to the most frequently occurring traits of Dreiser's characters, Rosenberg and Jones revealed various representational dimensions which were central in his life and personality (e.g., the idealization of unconventionality and the corresponding devaluation of conformity; see also Swanberg 1965). Since that preliminary study, Rosenberg has developed free-response procedures in which an individual characterizes persons whom he knows (100 or more), both in terms of the traits which he sees in them and the feelings they elicit in him, and various images of the self, e.g., the positive ideal self, the negative ideal self, the real self, etc. (See Rosenberg 1976 for further and technical detail.) Cluster and scaling analyses of protocols derived from these descriptions elucidate co-occurring trait and feeling attributions and provide a quasi-formal picture of the individual's subjectively construed social field. The capacity of these analyses not only to define more or less coherent clusters of attributions, but also to reveal the relationships among clusters (i.e., the degree to which they are positively or negatively correlated with one another), makes them especially valuable in personality research. Rosenberg's approach constitutes an alternate method for the study of the structures of the representational world and possesses a high degree of complementarity with traditional modes of psychobiographical research. His work thus deepens the investigation of the person and the study of the perception of the self in social psychology, while it introduces at the same time rigorously objective methods into the broader fields of intensive case analysis and personology.

Metapsychology and Empirical-Phenomenological Personality Research

One of the most important consequences of taking the representational world as the focus of personality psychology is the opportunity to systematically translate insoluble metapsychological problems into empirical-phenomenological research questions. As a first example, consider the problem of defining the ideal fulfillment of the human potential. As a metapsychological problem, this involves the determination of the universally optimum goal of personal development, the ultimate end-point toward which all human beings can be seen to be striving. It is, accordingly, speculative and incapable of being resolved on empirical grounds. In a framework oriented to the representational world, the quest for knowledge of the ultimate goal of human development is translated into empirical terms: the speculative problem of what *is* the ideal state for a human being to achieve is replaced by the researchable problem of *how* and *why* persons arrive at particular images of this ideal. To these questions our four studies already suggest a tentative answer; namely, that an individual's image of the ideal fulfillment of the human potential will represent his resolution of the subjective issues which have most deeply challenged his own capacity to adapt to the world. One thinks of the link between Freud's profound difficulties in relinquishing his mother's exclusive love and his rather embittered image of psychological maturity as involving the capacity to face the painful frustrations and renunciations required by civilized life. Or of Jung's vision of the achievement of transcendent wholeness, which was intimately tied to the deep division in his self-image. For Reich, the image of the ideal person (the so-called "genital character") was conceptualized in terms dramatically undoing his tragic attempt to suppress his beloved mother's sexuality, i.e., as a psychological state in which sexual life develops freely and without inhibition. And with Rank, the human ideal was formulated as the product of a successfully completed self-object differentiation and self-consolidation process, reflecting his own severe narcissistic struggles and difficulties. Such a funtional principle relating critical subjective dilemmas to images of the ideal human state is also potentially useful for the psychology of knowledge, particularly with reference to studies of utopian thinkers, educational theorists, and social philosophers (Tomkins 1963). It is furthermore a principle which might be validated on a large population, requiring only a means for determining the image of the ideal and the salient problematic issue for each person studied.

A second metapsychological problem that can be translated, concerns the establishing of the central dimensions of human personality along which individuals are seen to differ. This is the problem to which all typological systems are addressed, whether they arise from speculative reflection, clinical observation, or more structured methods, such as factor analysis. A psychology of personality which takes the representational world as its essential subject matter recognizes that the number of qualitative dimensions which can be used to conceptualize the diversity of persons is indefinitely large and that no empirical procedure can establish any subset of these dimensions as being centrally significant for all. Accordingly, the pursuit of universal typological and qualitative dimensional systems is eschewed. But again, a recognition of what this metapsychological issue conceals makes possible its translation into an empirical problem of great importance. While there may be no attainable universally valid system of human types, nevertheless each individual relates to others as if he possessed such a system. We interpret the metapsychological type-theories as manifestations of the general human tendency to categorize other persons in subjectively particularized ways. Thus we replace the speculative and empirically insoluble problem of defining the central dimensions of human personality by a set of research questions about the structuralization of the individual's subjective social field. We believe that the dimensions on which a person organizes his interpersonal world can be construed as externalizations of his own most salient experiential conflicts and concerns. This principle is illustrated by the explicit categories which personality theorists construct (e.g., introversion-extraversion in Jung; the neurotic, average man, and creative artist in Rank, etc.), but its applicability to others for whom such categories and dimensions remain wholly implicit and prereflective can also be studied. Rosenberg's (1976) methods of analysis would seem to be especially suited to the detection of such implicit dimensions.

Other divisive metapsychological issues and problems similarly can be translated and thereby used to enrich the field of personality research. As a last example, consider the recent "dispositionism-situationism" controversy (Mischel 1968, Bowers 1973), which revolves around the problem of the ultimate locus of causality in human behavior. "Dispositionists" envision the existence of stable internal traits or motivational trends which exert widely generalized causal effects on the person's overt actions. "Situationists," by contrast, emphasize the degree to which the causes of behavior are located in the stimulus conditions of the environment. Allied to the problem of identifying the efficacious causes of behavior is the issue of the stability or consistency of personality over time and across different situations. Dispositionists focus on the ways in which the individual's actions remain stable and regular regardless of external circumstances, whereas situationists stress the variability of behavior as a function of its environmental context. A psychology of personality oriented toward understanding the representational world is not concerned with localizing ultimate causes and tracing the flow of influence between the organism and the environment, for it reinterprets the categories of internal and external as subjective; they become regions of experience rather than regions of space. Thus the problem of the locus of causality, and the dynamics and directionality of its flow, can be treated in an empirical and phenomenological fashion, through studies of the various ways in which they are experienced (see Stolorow 1970, 1971). For some persons, their conduct is experienced as primarily under the control of the external world; indeed, there are experiences of such utter dependence upon the environment that the individual feels his identity changing as he moves from one external situation to another—for example, the "as-if" personalities whose identities change in chameleon-like fashion from one interpersonal context to the next (Helene Deutsch 1942). For many others, however, their conduct is experienced as always springing from within and as the product of personal intention and will; their sense of the continuity and stability of identity is accordingly less affected by alterations of the milieu. It seems to us that the dispositionism-situationism controversy may be rooted in such phenomenological differences.

One of the ideas which we have stressed is that human experience and conduct constitute the empirical domain of personality psychology. We use the term *conduct* rather than *behavior* because the latter carries connotations of physical action divested of subjective meanings, and a person's action, in our view, can only be understood if it is interpreted as embedded in an experiential field and as a response to a subjectively construed environment. One can, of course, analyze an individual's actions on a strictly physicalistic and objective plane, and study his actions' varied relationships to the physically stimulating conditions of the environment; but we would argue that such analyses are of questionable relevance to the domain of human issues with which personality psychology has classically been concerned.

Owing to its commitment to describing and accounting for phenomenological contents, a psychology of personality focused upon the representational world is involved primarily with the interpretation of the meanings implicit in the individual's experiences. It seeks to elucidate, both descriptively and genetically, the modes in which the person subjectively relates to himself, to others, and to the world at large. This approach does not treat personality as any kind of quasi-objective entity, nor is it particularly concerned with tracing the physical causality of behavior; furthermore, it does not require a foundation on biological or neurophysiological hypotheses and models.[1] It is an independent empirical discipline possessing its own methods of inquiry and its own conceptual language of phenomenological and psychological terms.

Two themes are intertwined in this book, one pertaining to the subjectivity of psychological knowledge, and the other to the encapsulating metapsychological doctrines which we believe have hindered the development of personality psychology as a unified discipline. By analyzing the subjective origins of four major personality theories, we have attempted to show how their metapsychological concepts reflect the particularized personal viewpoints of their creators. Our studies have led us to make some proposals for a metapsychology-free conceptual framework oriented toward the subjective representational world of the individual. Within such a framework, a psychoanalytic phenomenology becomes possible in which the unique contributions of the different theorists can be reformulated and integrated. Furthermore, a consistent focus on the representational world can be shown to have a variety of important implications for psychodiagnosis, psychoanalytic therapy, and the broader field of personality theory and research.

NOTE

1. To say that the psychology of the representational world constitutes a conceptual domain which is distinct from biological thought is obviously not to claim that no relationships between the two exist. A wide range of biological and physiological conditions may have a profound impact on the individual's subjective representational world. These conditions include, for example, the maturation of neurological structures, various neurological deficits and disturbances, biochemical imbalances and sensitivities. The study of the impact of such conditions on the representational world is another intriguing area of research.

REFERENCES

Ansbacher, H., and Ansbacher, R., eds. (1956). *The Individual Psychology of Alfred Adler*. New York: Harper and Row.

Apfelbaum, B. (1965). Ego psychology, psychic energy, and the hazards of quantitative explanation in psychoanalytic theory. *International Journal of Psycho-Analysis* 46:168–182.

Arlow, J. (1975). The structural hypothesis—theoretical considerations. *Psychoanalytic Quarterly* 44:509–525.

Atkin, S. (1975). Ego synthesis and cognition in a borderline case. *Psychoanalytic Quarterly* 44:29–61.

Basch, M. (1976). Theory formation in chapter VII: a critique. *Journal of American Psychoanalytic Association* 24:61–100.

Bowers, K. (1973). Situationism in psychology: an analysis and a critique. *Psychological Review* 80:307–336.

Burgner, M., and Edgcumbe, R. (1972). Some problems in the conceptualization of early object relationships. Part II: the concept of object constancy. *Psychoanalytic Study of the Child* 27:315–333.

Carlson, R. (1971). Where is the person in personality research? *Psychological Bulletin* 75:203–219.

Dahl, H., reporter (1968). Panel on 'psychoanalytic theory of the instinctual drives in relation to recent developments.' *Journal of the American Psychoanalytic Association* 16:627–632.

Deutsch, H. (1942). Some forms of emotional disturbances and their relationship to schizophrenia. *Psychoanalytic Quarterly* 11:301–321.

Ehrenwald, J. (1966). *Psychotherapy: Myth and Method*. New York: Grune and Stratton.

Erikson, E. (1956). The problem of ego identity. In *Identity and the Life Cycle*. Psychological Issues Monograph No. 1, pp. 101–171. New York: International Universities Press, 1959.

Fairbairn, W. (1952). *An Object-Relations Theory of the Personality*. New York: Basic Books, 1954.

Freud, A. (1937). *The Ego and the Mechanisms of Defense*. New York: International Universities Press, 1946.

Freud, S. (1915). Instincts and their vicissitudes. *Standard Edition* 14:117–140. London: Hogarth Press, 1957.

—— (1917 [1915]). Mourning and melancholia. *Standard Edition* 14:243–258. London: Hogarth Press, 1957.

Fromm, E. (1941). *Escape From Freedom.* New York: Avon, 1965.

Gill, M. (1976). Metapsychology is not psychology. In *Psychology versus Metapsychology: Psycho-Analytic Essays in Memory of George S. Klein.* Psychological Issues Monograph No. 36, ed. M. Gill and P. Holzman, pp. 71–105. New York: International Universities Press.

Gill, M., and Holzman, P.' (1976). *Psychology versus Metapsychology: Psychoanalytic Essays in Memory of George S. Klein* Psychological Issues Monograph No. 36. New York: International Universities Press.

Guntrip, H. (1969). *Schizoid Phenomena, Object-Relations and the Self.* New York: International Universities Press.

Holt, R. (1965). A review of some of Freud's biological assumptions and their influence on his theories. In *Psychoanalysis and Current Biological Thought,* ed. N. Greenfield and W. Lewis, pp. 93–124. Madison: University of Wisconsin Press.

—— (1967). Beyond vitalism and mechanism: Freud's concept of psychic energy. *Science and Psychoanalysis* 11:1–41. New York: Grune and Stratton.

—— (1975). The past and future of ego psychology. *Psychoanalytic Quarterly* 44:550–576.

—— (1976). Drive or wish? A reconsideration of the psychoanalytic theory of motivation. In *Psychology versus Metapsychology: Psychoanalytic Essays in Memory of George S. Klein.* Psychological Issues Monograph No. 36, ed. M. Gill and P. Holzman, pp. 158–197. New York: International Universities Press.

Holzman, P. (1976). Theoretical models and the treatment of the schizophrenias. In *Psychology versus Metapsychology: Psychoanalytic Essays in Memory of George S. Klein.* Psychological Issues Monograph No. 36, ed. M. Gill and P. Holzman, pp. 134–157. New York: International Universities Press.

Home, H. (1966). The concept of the mind. *International Journal of Psycho-Analysis* 47:42–49.

Horney, K. (1950). *Neurosis and Human Growth.* New York: W. W. Norton.

Jacobson, E. (1957). Denial and repression. *Journal of the American Psychoanalytic Association* 5:61–92.

—— (1964). *The Self and the Object World.* New York: International Universities Press.

Kernberg, O. (1975). *Borderline Conditions and Pathological Narcissism.* New York: Jason Aronson.

Klein, G. (1976). *Psychoanalytic Theory: An Exploration of Essentials.* New York: International Universities Press.

Kohut, H. (1971). *The Analysis of the Self.* New York: International Universities Press.

Kubie, L. (1947). The fallacious use of quantitative concepts in dynamic psychology. *Psychoanalytic Quarterly* 16:507–518.

—— (1975). The language tools of psychoanalysis: a search for better tools drawn from better models. *International Review of Psycho-Analysis* 2:11–24.

Mahler, M., Pine, F., and Bergman, A. (1975). *The Psychological Birth of the Human Infant.* New York: Basic Books.

Mischel, W. (1968). *Personality and Assessment.* New York: John Wiley.

Peterfreund, E. (1971). *Information, Systems and Psychoanalysis: An Evolutionary Biological Approach to Psychoanalytic Theory.* Psychological Issues Monograph No. 25/26. New York: International Universities Press.

—— (1975). The need for a new general theoretical frame of reference for psychoanalysis. *Psychoanalytic Quarterly* 44:534–549.

Piaget, J. (1937). *The Construction of Reality in the Child.* New York: Basic Books.

Pulver, S. (1970). Narcissism: the term and the concept. *Journal of the American Psychoanalytic Association* 18:319–341.

Rosenberg, S. (1976). New approaches to the analysis of personal constructs in person perception. *Nebraska Symposium on Motivation 23.* Lincoln: University of Nebraska Press.

Rosenberg, S., and Jones, R. (1972). A method for investigating and representing a person's implicit theory of personality: Theodore Dreiser's view of people. *Journal of Personality and Social Psychology* 22:372–386.

Rubinstein, B. (1967). Explanation and mere description: a

metascientific examination of certain aspects of the psychoanalytic theory of motivation. In *Motives and Thought: Psychoanalytic Essays in Honor of David Rapaport.* Psychological Issues Monograph No. 18/19, ed. R. Holt, pp. 20–77. New York: International Universities Press.

——— (1976). On the possibility of a strictly clinical psychoanalytic theory: an essay in the philosophy of psychoanalysis. In *Psychology versus Metapsychology: Psychoanalytic Essays in Memory of George S. Klein.* Psychological Issues Monograph No. 36, ed. M. Gill and P. Holzman, pp. 229–264. New York: International Universities Press.

Sandler, A. M. (1975). Comments on the significance of Piaget's work for psychoanalysis. *International Review of Psycho-Analysis* 2:365–377.

Sandler, J., and Joffe, W. (1969). Towards a basic psychoanalytic model. *International Journal of Psycho-Analysis* 50:79–90.

Sandler, J., and Rosenblatt, B. (1962). The concept of the representational world. *Psychoanalytic Study of the Child* 17:128–145.

Schafer, R. (1968). *Aspects of Internalization.* New York: International Universities Press.

——— (1972). Internalization: process or fantasy? *Psychoanalytic Study of the Child* 27:411–436.

——— (1973). Action: its place in psychoanalytic interpretation and theory. *Annual of Psychoanalysis* 1:159–196.

——— (1975). Psychoanalysis without psychodynamics. *International Journal of Psycho-Analysis* 56:41–55.

——— (1976). Emotion in the language of action. In *Psychology versus Metapsychology: Psychoanalytic Essays in Memory of George S. Klein.* Psychological Issues Monograph No. 36, ed. M. Gill and P. Holzman, pp. 106–133. New York: International Universities Press.

Searles, H. (1959). Integration and differentiation in schizophrenia: an over-all view. *British Journal of Medical Psychology* 32:261–281.

Stolorow, R. (1970). Mythic consonance and dissonance in the vicissitudes of transference. *American Journal of Psychoanalysis* 30:178–179.

—————— (1971). Causality-interpretation and obsessive versus hysterical functioning. *Journal of Personality Assessment* 35:32–37.

—————— (1975a). Toward a functional definition of narcissism. *International Journal of Psycho-Analysis* 56:179–185.

—————— (1975b). The narcissistic function of masochism (and sadism). *International Journal of Psycho-Analysis* 56:441–448.

Stolorow, R., and Lachmann, F. (1975). Early object loss and denial: developmental considerations. *Psychoanalytic Quarterly* 44:596–611.

—————— (1978). The developmental prestages of defenses: diagnostic and therapeutic implications. *Psychoanalytic Quarterly* 47:73–102.

Sullivan, H. (1953). *The Interpersonal Theory of Psychiatry.* New York: W. W. Norton.

Swanberg, W. (1965). *Dreiser.* New York: Scribners.

Tausk, V. (1919). On the origin of the 'influencing machine' in schizophrenia. *Psychoanalytic Quarterly* 2 (1933): 519–552.

Tomkins, S. (1962, 1963). *Affect, Imagery, Consciousness* (2 vols.). New York: Springer.

Waelder, R. (1936). The principle of multiple function: observations on over-determination. *Psychoanalytic Quarterly* 5:45–62.

Whitehead, C. (1975). Additional aspects of the Freudian-Kleinian controversy: towards a 'psychoanalysis' of psychoanalysis. *International Journal of Psycho-Analysis* 56:383–396.

Yankelovich, D., and Barrett, W. (1970). *Ego and Instinct.* New York: Random House.

INDEX

"action language," 77
adaptive function, in psychoana-
    lytic phenomenology, 184
Adelson, J., 35
Adler, A., 84, 166, 195
Ansbacher, H., 195
Ansbacher, R., 195
Apfelbaum, B., 174
archetype, collective unconscious
    and, 74–80
Arlow, J., 174, 175
artist, theme of, in work of Rank,
    147–50
Atkin S., 189
Atwood, G., 19, 104, 126, 167

Bach, S., 97
Bannister, D., 35
Barrett, W., 174
Basch, M., 174

behavior
    concept of, 202
    as science, 30
behaviorism, as circumvention of
    subjectivity, 29–33
Bergman, A., 86, 134, 186, 187
Bernays, Martha (Martha Freud),
    55
Binswanger, L., 39, 43
"biological core," 113
biological research, treatment of
    cancer and, 116–18
birth trauma, in work of Rank,
    132–34
Boadella, D., 111, 118
Bowers, K., 201
"bracketing," in phenomenology,
    37
Breuer, J., 60, 62
Brücke, E., 174

Bruner, G., 41
Bruno, 128
Burgner, M., 187, 188
Buss, A., 25

cancer, treatment of, biological research and 116–18
Carlson, R., 35, 196
case study method, in subjectivity, personality theory and metapsychology, 39–44
representational world and, 42–44
character analysis, as thematic structure in Reich's work, 112–13
character structure, 183
Charcot, Jean, 56
childhood traumata, in life of Rank, 163–64
Chomsky, N., 28
circumventions, attempted, of subjectivity, 29–39
behaviorism, 29–33
methodological objectivism, 33–36
phenomenology, 36–39
civilization, Reich's image of, 124–28
Coan, R., 19
cognitive-emotional schemata, 178, 183
collective unconscious, archetypes, and, 74–80
Communist Party involvement of Reich, 115, 116
conduct, concept of, 202
correlates, objective, 32

Dahl, H., 174
Darwin, C., 161
deadly orgone energy (DOR), 127
decentering, in genesis of knowledge, 26–29
"deep structure" of language, 28
defenses, common, in psychoanalytic phenomenology, 189–91
represssion, denial and, 189–90
defensive function, in psychoanalytic phenomenology, 185
defensive-restitutive function of Freud's theories, 63–68
denial, as defense in psychoanalytic phenomenology, 189–91
Descartes, René, 36
Deutsch, H., 87, 202
developmental origins, psychoanalytic phenomenology and, 183
differentiation, representational, in psychoanalytic phenomenology, 187–89
displacement, as defense in psycho-analytic phenomenology, 191
"dispositionism-situationism" controversy, 201–202
disunited man, in Jung's theories, 83–85
double, concept of, in Rank's work, 136–38
Dreiser, T., 198

Edgcumbe, R., 187, 188
Ehrenwald, J., 181

"eidetic essences," Husserl's notion of, 38
empirical-phenomenological personality research, metapsychology and, 199–203
enantiodromia, in Jung's theories, 84, 85
Engels, Frederick, 114
Erikson, E., 25, 55, 188
experience, phenomenological, 31
extrinsic perspectives on knowledge, 24

Fairbairn, W., 186
Fine, R., 63
Fliess, Wilhelm, 49, 50, 54, 60, 61, 62, 63, 64
Food and Drug Administration, 127
Freud, Anna (daughter), 190
Freud, Anna (sister), 50, 51, 54, 58, 69
Freud, Emanuel, 49
Freud, John, 49, 53, 68
Freud, Julius, 49, 52, 54, 58, 66
Freud, Martha, 54, 56, 57, 58, 59, 60, 61, 63, 64
Freud, Philipp, 49, 51
Freud, Sigmund, 15, 16, 18, 23, 25, 26, 41, 47–69, 84, 99, 100, 103, 112, 114, 123, 124, 156, 161, 165, 166, 167, 174, 175, 179, 180, 182, 184, 185, 186, 191, 195, 199–20
  adult relationships, 54–63
  ambivalence in life of, 48–54
  earliest experiences, 49–54

Civilization and its Discontents, 68
defensive-restitutive function of theories, 63–68
Interpretation of Dreams, The, 53
New Introductory Lectures, 65–66
summary and conclusions, 68–69
Fromm, E., 195
functional significance, psychoanalytic phenomenology and, 183

Galileo, 128
genesis of knowledge, decentering in, 26–29
Gill, M., 174, 177, 178, 179
Goethe, J.W. von, 55
Goldberg, A., 131
Gouldner, A., 28
Guntrip, H., 186

Helmholtz, H.L.F., 174
hero, myth of birth of, in Rank's work, 134–36
Higgins, M., 123, 124
history, Reich's image of, 124–28
Holt, R., 174, 175
Holzman, P., 174, 175
Home, H., 177, 178, 179
Horney, K., 195
Husserl, E., 36, 37–38, 39

Ibsen, H., 161
immanent perspectives on knowledge, 24

incorporation, as defense in psychoanalytic phenomenology, 191
individuation, in Jung's theories, 85–89
integration, representational, in psychoanalytic phenomenology, 187–89
International Psychoanalytic Association, 116, 123, 124
isolation
as defense in psychoanalytic phenomenology, 191
splendid, in life of Rank, 156–60

Jacobson, E., 134, 186, 187, 188, 189
Jesus Christ, Reich's fascination with historical figure of, 124, 125, 128
Joffe, W., 178
Jones, E., 48, 51, 55, 56, 57, 58, 59, 60, 61, 69
Jones, R., 198
Judas Iscariot, Reich's fascination with Christ and, 125
Jung, Carl, 15, 16, 18, 23, 25, 41, 73–107, 17;, 180, 181, 184–85, 189, 195, 200, 201
Answer to Job, 93
Memories, Dreams, Reflections, 90
psychological origins of theories, 90–107
experiences, critical formative, 100–103

secret, genesis of, 90–100
subjectivity and, 103–107
representational world in theories of, 73–89
collective unconscious, archetype and, 74–80
disunited man, 83–85
individuation, 85–89
self-dissolution, 80–83
summary and conclusions, 107
Two Essays on Analytic Psychology, 74

Kant, I., 36
Kelly, 35, 43
Kernberg, O., 77, 136, 186, 188, 189, 191
Klein, G., 174, 175, 177, 178, 179, 182, 183, 184, 185, 186
knowledge
genesis of, decentering in, 26–29
psychology and sociology of, 23–26
Kohut, H., 61, 77, 81, 88, 131, 134, 135, 137, 139, 141, 143, 144, 146, 147, 149, 169, 186, 188, 189
Kubie, L., 174, 175, 176

Lachmann, F., 77, 185, 189, 193
language, "deep structure" of, 28
Levenson, E., 25
Lifton, R., 25
Locke, John, 38
"lost paradise," Rank's notion of, 132, 133

McGuire, W., 34, 103

Mahler, M., 86, 134, 186, 187
Mair, J., 35
man, disunited, in Jung's theories, 83–85
Mannheim, K., 23, 24, 25, 28
Marx, Karl, 24, 28, 114, 123
Mazlish, B., 25
metapsychology
    definition of, 174
    empirical-phenomenological personality research and, 199–203
    psychoanalytic, critiques of, 174–79
    representational world and, 179–82
    See also subjectivity, personality theory and metapsychology
methodological objectivism, 33–36
Meyer, M., 57
Meynert, T., 174
Mischel, W., 201
mood disorder, in life of Rank, 151–56
Murray, H., 39

Napoleon Bonaparte, 161
narcissitic disturbance, evidence of, in life of Rank, 151–63
    mood disorder, 151–56
    object relations, 160–63
    splendid isolation, 156–60
narcissistic love, in work of Rank, 140–44
nature, Reich's image of, 124–28
Newton, Isaac, 27
Nietzsche, Friedrich, 154, 161, 165, 166

Nin, Anais, 162, 163

objective correlates, 32
objectivism, methodological, 33–36
object relations, in life of Rank, 160–63
observer, as observed, 17–29
    genesis of knowledge, decentering in, 26–29
    psychology and sociology of knowledge, 23–26
    validity and subjectivity of, 21–24
Oedipus complex, Freud's notion of, 41, 53, 64
orgastic potency, as thematic structure in Reich's work, 112–13
orgone energy (OR), 127

personality research, 196–97
    empirical-phenomenological metapsychology and, 199–203
personality structure, 183
personality theory. *See* subjectivity, personality theory and metapsychology
"person perception," Rosenberg's notion of, 197–98
Peterfreund, E., 174, 175, 176
phenomenological-empirical personality research, metapsychology and, 199–203
phenomenological experience, 31

phenomenological reduction, Husserl's notion of, 36
phenomenology, 36–39
  "bracketing," 37–38
  psychoanalytic. *See* psychoanalytic phenomenology, psychology of representational world and
Piaget, J., 26, 27, 43, 187
Pine, F., 86, 134, 186, 187
Polanyi, M., 35
"primary narcissism," 134
projection, as defense in psychoanalytic phenomenology, 191
"protoneurophysiology," Rubinstein's notion of, 176
psychoanalytic phenomenology, psychology of representational world and, 173–203
  critiques of psychoanalytic metapsychology, 174–79
  establishing as discipline, efforts toward, 182–91
    adaptive function, 184
    common defenses, 189–91
    defensive function, 185
    representational differentiation and integration, 187–89
    restitutive-reparative function, 184–85
    self-guiding and self-punishing function, 184
    wish-fulfilling function, 184
  implications, 192–203
    metapsychology, empirical-phenomenological person-
    ality research, 199–203
    personality research, 196–97
    psychoanalytic therapy, 193–94
    psychodiagnosis, 192–93
    representational world, procedure for exploring, 197–99
    schools of psychoanalytic thought, 194–95
  metapsychology, representational world and, 179–82
psychoanalytic therapy, 193–94
psychoanalytic thought, schools of, 194–95
psychodiagnosis, 192–93
psycho-history, 25
psychological origins of Jung's theories, 90–107
  experiences, critical formative, 100–103
  secret, genesis of, 90–100
  subjectivity and, 103–107
psychology of knowledge, 23–26
psychology of representational world, psychoanalytic phenomenology and. *See* psychoanalytic phenomenology, psychology of representational world and
Pulver, S., 175

Rank, Otto, 16, 23, 41, 131–70, 179, 180, 185, 189, 195, 200, 201
  Art and Artist, 149
  Beyond Psychology, 142, 149, 162, 169
  "Daybooks," 133, 154, 155, 156, 158, 160, 163, 165, 169

Double, The, 136, 137
  life of, 150–69
  childhood traumata, 163–64
  narcissistic disturbance, evidence of, 151–63
  reparative trends, 164–67
  subjectivity in theories of, 167–69
Myth of the Birth of the Hero, The, 135, 136
Psychology and the Soul, 140, 142, 169
  summary and conclusions, 169–70
Trauma of Birth, The, 132, 133,
Truth and Reality, 133, 138, 139, 143
Will Therapy, 133, 138, 139, 141, 146
  work of, notions in, 132–50
  artist, theme of, 147–50
  birth trauma, 132–34
  double, concept of, 136–38
  hero, the, 134–36
  narcissistic love, 140–44
  sexual dread, self-dissolution and, 144–47
  will, concept of, 138–40
Raphael, C., 123, 124
reaction formation, as defense in psychoanalytic phenomenology, 191
reduction, phenomenological, Husserl's notion of, 36
Reich, Ilse Ollendorff, 119, 120, 121, 123, 128
Reich, Peter, 118, 128
Reich, Robert, 119

Reich, Wilhelm, 15, 16, 23, 25, 26, 41, 111–28, 179, 180, 181, 185, 195, 200
Book of Dreams, A, 118
Cancer Biopathy, The, 117
Character Analysis, 113
  childhood trauma, pivotal, 119–22
Cosmic Superimposition, 126
Ether, God and Devil, 125
"Imposition of Sexual Morality, The," 114
  life and thought, aspects of, 122–28
  history, civilization and nature, images of, 124–28
Mass Psychology of Fascism, The, 115
Murder of Christ, The, 124
  summary and conclusions, 128
  work, thematic structure of, 112–19
  biological research, treatment of cancer and, 116–18
  character analysis, orgastic potency and, 112–13
  political thought, 113–16
  unidentified flying objects (UFOs), 118–19
reparative trends, in life of Rank, 164–67
representational world
  in case study method, 42–44
  in Jung's theories, 73–89
  collective unconscious, archetype and, 74–80
  disunited man, 83–85
  individualism, 85–89

self-dissolution, 80–83
metapsychology and, 179–82
procedure for exploring, 197–99
psychology of. *See* psychoanalytic phenomenology, psychology of representational world and repression, as defense in psychoanlytic phenomenology, 189–91
restitutive-defensive function of Freud's theories, 63–68
restitutive-reparative function, in psychoanalytic phenomenology, 184–85
Rie, O., 62
Rosenberg, S., 197, 198, 199, 201
Rosenblatt, B., 42, 182
Rousseau, J.J., 27
Rubinstein, B., 174, 175, 176
Rycroft, C., 111

Sandler, J., 42, 178, 182, 187
Sartre, J.P., 19, 39
Schafer, R., 177, 178, 179, 182, 190
schools of psychoanalytic thought, 194–95
Schopenhauer, Arthur, 161, 165
Schur, M., 50, 60, 61, 62
Schweitzer, Albert, 124
Searles, H., 188
Sechrest, L., 36
secret, genesis of, in psychological origins of Jung's theories, 90–107
self-dissolution
in Jung's theories, 80–83
sexual dread and, in work of Rank, 144–47

self-guiding function, in psychoanalytic phenomenology, 184
self-object, transitional, 97
self-punishing function, in psychoanalytic phenomenology, 184
sexual dread, self-dissolution and, in work of Rank, 144–47
"situationism-dispositionism" controversery, 201–202
Skinner, B.F., 30, 31, 32, 33
Smith, M., 41
sociology of knowledge, 23–26
Socrates, 128
splendid isolation, in life of Rank, 156–60
splitting, as defense in psychoanalytic phenomenology, 191
stasis, of sexuality, Reich's notion of, 112
Stolorow, R., 77, 80, 126, 131, 137, 139, 143, 144, 164, 175, 182, 185, 188, 189, 193, 202
structure, thematic, of Reich's work, 112–19
biological research, treatment of cancer and, 116–18
character analysis, orgastic potency and, 112–13
political thought, 113–16
unidentified flying objects (UFOs), 118–19
subjectivity, personality theory and metapsychology, 15–44
case study method and, 39–44
representational world, 42–44
circumventions, attempted, of

subjectivity, 29–39
  behaviorism, 29–33
  methodological objectivism,
    33–36
  phenomenology, 36–39
in Jung's theories, 103–107
observer, as observed, 17–29
  genesis of knowledge, decen-
    tering in, 26–29
  psychology and sociology of
    knowledge, 23–26
  validity and subjectivity of,
    21–23
subjectivity, in theories of Rank,
  167–69
Sullivan, H., 188, 195
Swanberg, W., 198

Taft, J., 133, 147, 150, 151, 152,
  156, 157, 158, 159, 160, 162,
  163, 164, 166, 169
Tausk, V., 188
"theorectomy," of psychoanalysis,
  Klein's notion of, 178
Titchener, E., 29
Tomkins, S., 19, 24, 64–65, 66, 67,
  104, 167, 186, 200
"transcendental subjectivity," Husserl's notion of, 36
transitional self-object, 97

unidentified flying objects (UFOs),
  in work of Reich, 118–19

validity and subjectivity, of observer as observed, 21–23
Van Kaam, A., 39

Waelder, R., 185
Wagner, R., 161
Wahle, F., 58
Weber, M., 24
White, R., 39, 41
Whitehead, C., 194
will, concept of, in work of Rank,
  138–40
"will psychology," Rank's notion
  of, 138, 140
"will to power," Adler's notion of,
  84, 104
wish-fulfilling function, in psychoanalytic phenomenol-
  ogy, 184
"world-design," Binswanger's notion of, 43
Wundt, W., 29
Wycoff, J., 111

Yankelovich, D., 174

Zetzel, E., 68